# Going About!

## A WATERWAY ADVENTURE

### GILLIAN OUTERBRIDGE

## The Nautical Publishing Company
An Imprint of Far Horizons Media Company

Far Horizons Media Company is a division of NetPV, Inc.

*Gillian Outerbridge*

Published by
The Nautical Publishing Company
www.NauticalPublishing.com

An Imprint of Far Horizons Media Company
www.FarHorizonsMedia.com

Far Horizons Media Company is a Division of NetPV, Inc.
P. O. Box 560989, Rockledge, FL 32956 - www.NetPV.com

Please note that charts in this book are for illustration only and are not intended for navigation.

ISBN:    978-0-9789350-2-3

LCCN:    2007922803

# Dedication

*Dedicated to esteemed friends*
*Lin and Larry Pardey*
*whose motto*
*"go small, go simple, go now"*
*were just the words I needed to hear.*

# Appreciation

*Grateful thanks to Lois Gilbert for her*
*assistance in manuscript preparation.*

# CONTENTS

> ### Going About! –
>
> *"The warning to a boat crew that the skipper is about to change direction."*

# INTRODUCTION

Gillian, aged 20, moved from London to Bermuda to save enough money to buy a small boat and sail from the U.K. to the Greek Islands. Forty years later, a near tragic event encouraged her to belatedly embark on her life's dream.

She set sail in her 20-foot sloop *Dart*—destination Greece, NY. Instead of the Mediterranean, she chose the tranquil inland waterways of New York State and Canada.

Through locks and lakes, rivers and canals, she and her devoted Jack Russell terrier Tucker navigated thousands of miles of serene waterways. She and Tucker enjoyed adventures and achievements, conquered fears, and made new friends.

On returning home, she realized it was not yet time to "retire" and has since purchased a small motor vessel, *Patience*, a Maple Bay 27, to continue her voyaging.

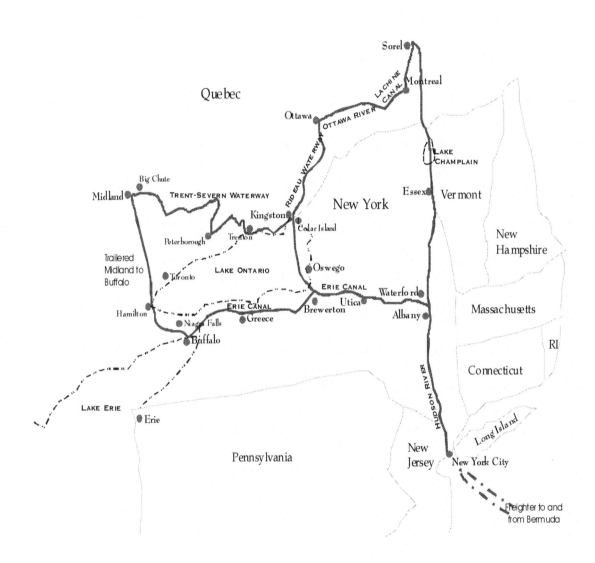

# CHAPTER ONE

# Second Chance

"Now that you've been given your life back, what are you going to do with it?" The question startled and disturbed me. I staggered back, psychologically that is, since I was seated deep in a spacious armchair. Across from me, also in a comfortable chair, sat Sarah, my counselor and mentor, elegantly clad as always in a long, cream linen shift and dramatic, dangling earrings, gazing benignly at me.

A miniature angel in a small woven hammock swung gently against the window that framed the brilliant aquamarine of Hamilton Harbour in Bermuda, my home for 40 years. I knew Sarah's mild gaze concealed a quick wit and perceptive mind, but the question came as a surprise. I came here to her consulting room today for solace, for professional guidance, for sympathy, and for some psyche-stroking, not to be put on the spot.

I had phoned her, my voice shaking with emotion, and she had kindly agreed to meet with me at once to hear my tale of terror.

"What am I going to do with my life?"

I mulled and mused to myself, thinking, "Can't we just deal with now and with what I am just coping with? I can't handle the future yet!"

Sarah lobbed another pointed question across the room. "What's the worst thing you could ever have imagined happening to you?" I recognized the loaded question but had my answer ready. "To wake up in the night, naked and alone in my bed, and find a masked man holding a hunting knife at my throat."

"OK," she replied with an air of mild triumph. "Just think of this. You have already experienced the worst you could imagine, and you survived."

Clever Sarah. How quickly she turned me from victim to survivor. I wasn't going to be allowed to dwell on the ghastly attack that left me traumatized. I recalled the terrifying moment when a slight noise woke me in the predawn gloom, and I saw, across my bedroom, a man, clothed and

1

hooded in black, brandishing a fearsome hunting knife. "No!" I wailed. "No! No!"

In an instant, he loomed grimly above me, and suddenly his left hand was clamped across my mouth, and the gleaming blade was poised over my head.

"I'm dead!" was the first thought that raced through my mind. The second was to get hold of the knife, and I reached up both hands toward the vicious weapon. My mind seemed to operate on two levels. One was a blind panic, struggling for survival. The other was coolheaded and rational, advising me calmly to remember what I'd learned. Don't just shout help, shout rape, murder, police. Call your neighbors by name. Make as much noise as you can. Use your feet as weapons! I began a furious battle. I thrashed my head from under his hand and yelled and kicked while both hands gripped the wrist that held the knife. I shouted, "Help! Rape! Murder! Call the police! Call the police!"

As I fought, I searched mentally for a weapon, then swept the large model pond yacht from my bedside table and held it against my chest. My attacker, who had remained silent throughout the fight, stepped back, gave a pointed shrug of exasperation, and strode unceremoniously out of my bedroom and out of the apartment. By this time, neighbors had heard my cries and were running to my rescue. Months of nightmares and flashbacks eventually dwindled, but when I talked with Sarah that day, the event was still horribly clear in my mind.

"Now that you've been given your life back, what are you going to do with it?" I suspect Sarah already knew what my answer would be. She had come to know me well during the past months of relationship counseling.

"What am I going to do with my life?" I answered. "What I've always wanted to do—I'm going cruising."

An image of my Pacific Seacraft Flicka 20 *Dart* floated briefly across my inner vision. She was moored nearby in a sheltered cove where she tugged gently at her nylon bridle like a compliant pony. I had bought her years ago, and she later came to me in the divorce. She was capable of voyaging the oceans of the world, but I was quite happy sailing her around the local harbor. Not content with generalities, Sarah pulled her note pad onto her knee and started planning my future by firing questions and writing down the answers. "Where will you go? How will you get your boat there? Who is the shipping agent? What do you need to do to get the boat ready?"

*I was quite happy sailing her around the local harbor.*

Within the allotted hour of counseling time, a chart of my immediate future had been mapped out for me. Clutching the pages torn from Sarah's yellow note pad, I floated out of her office feeling a heck of a lot better than when I went in. It was not the nicest way to make a life change, not the kindest of "wake-up calls," but it had the desired effect.

How many years had I dreamed of such an adventure and almost lost the opportunity? Where had 40 years gone? No, more than 40—50 at least. The waterways of the world had been calling to me since childhood, and I had pretty much ignored the calls. At the age of six, I sailed a primitive wooden raft in the shallow pools left by the receding tide on the mile-wide rippled sands of Blackpool Beach and watched my proud, small craft pushed by a fitful breeze toward a distant horizon.

I dragged my amenable grandfather onto chilly, English sailing ponds to pedal or paddle or row rental craft for an hour, both of us bundled in warm jackets and shivering, he with cold and I with excitement. I once stood with my grandfather on the bank of a canal near his home in the industrial north of England while we waited for the passing of a canal boat. All of 70 feet long and laden with coal, the barge almost filled the narrow canal. As it glided past us, a sturdy woman leaning her weight on the long, steel tiller gave us a cheery wave as they rounded the gentle curve.

The living cabin only occupied a few feet at the stern of the barge, and the sides were brightly painted in primary colors with flowers, birds, and a magnificent castle. Through the small windows, shaded with net curtains, a couple of young children shyly peeked. A black and white terrier barked briefly and ran along the top of the laden barge as they passed.

Holding one of my home-made craft in my small hand, I questioned Grandpa. "Who are these people? Where are they going? Do they live on the boat? Do the children go to school?"

Imagine, I thought, your home taking you to new surroundings, not just every day, but every hour. A different view from the window every few minutes. A traveling home.

I remembered a Sunday afternoon on a winter day in England when, as a teenager, I settled by the glowing, coal fire with the family, teacups rattling in their saucers, butter melting on toasted crumpets, reading in the newspaper a review of a small motorboat complete with galley, head, and berths which was "ideal to cruise through the European inland waterways to Greece." Ah, Greece! Ernle Bradford's evocative book *The Journeying Moon*, describing his voyage through Europe to Greece on the Dutch boeier *Mother Goose*, inspired me to plan a similar voyage.

A couple of years later, I had the opportunity to join relatives in Bermuda where, my cousins assured me, I could save enough money for a boat to take me to Greece, certainly much faster than I could do so sharing a basement flat in a dingy part of London where I earned the equivalent of $10 per week, with overheads of $11 per week.

A few years later, I quite thought my new, young, Bermudian husband George was equally intrigued by the idea of cruising through Europe. I guess we were living on different planets (Mars and Venus, probably) as even 40 years later, he still claims that he had no idea what I had in mind.

The years swept past quickly like the fierce currents that orbit the oceans. I flew through the years of motherhood, the decades of wifely duties, the "committee years" of middle age, and the commitments of the family boat charter business. The calls to the sea had echoed in the back of my mind, but the boats diminished in size as the decades passed.

When I was 20, I hankered after a 60-foot Baltic Trader. At 30, I greedily eyed a 50-foot, red-hulled Canadian schooner for sale in the local harbor. In my forties, I tugged my husband and two small but enthusiastic daughters off to England to consider a 40-foot Salar sloop languishing at a wind-swept marina in Brighton.

I was approaching 50 and still boatless when a friend and fellow-boater dropped off to me an old copy of *Small Boat Journal*. "There's the boat for you," said Don. "A Flicka." I loved the sound of the stout little craft, designed by Bruce Bingham. It was modeled after the sturdy Newport lobster boats that sailed out of Rhode Island at the turn of the century. Bingham was impressed by their ability to handle rough weather, yet provide enough accommodation to stay at sea for days. It was many years later that he developed the design of the popular mini-yacht known world-wide and built by Pacific Seacraft. He and Katie Burke eventually owned their own 20-foot Flicka *Sabrina*, and Bruce claimed, "Of all my designs, the Flicka remains my greatest source of pride."

Having made the decision to buy a Flicka, with husband George's blessing, I flew to the United States to view prospective purchases. In a quick trip, I looked at four Flickas, a kind of marine speed-dating, but when I saw *Dart*, I loved her at once. My family enjoyed sailing outings, swimming picnics, and cocktail cruises for many years, and when the divorce became final, *Dart* was on my side of the list of possessions being divided up.

# CHAPTER TWO

## North with Henry Hudson

There was a chilly bite to the northerly wind. Waves were starting to slap ruthlessly at *Dart's* cream-colored fiberglass hull as the small outboard engine steadily pushed us up the Hudson River. *Dart* heaved across the rolling waves that tumbled down the river. Clouds of mist swirled around the gloomy, green slopes of Bear Mountain. It was an exhilarating moment for me, a grandmother, a would-be adventurer, a neophyte explorer, joining the multitudes who had preceded me through the centuries.

*I was aboard my little boat in New York City, and
my Jack Russell terrier, Tucker, was perched on the cabin top.*

I felt the presence of the ghosts of mariners past, of fragile birch-bark canoes, sturdy timber schooners, of steam powered paddle wheelers, barges and freighters traveling into the interior, migrating through the rivers, and building canals to reach the West. I thought of Henry Hudson steering his way north and charting a route for the colonists and settlers who would follow, ready to change the face of America. I didn't want to change the face of America, just savor it.

A ragged group of gulls coasted overhead, and not far away a posse of mallard ducks drifted dejectedly in a scattered rank. Only hours earlier, I had cheered myself as I motored my Flicka *Dart* past the sunlit Manhattan skyline. My spirits were high. I was aboard my little boat in New York City, and my Jack Russell terrier, Tucker, was perched on the cabin top. She loved being on board *Dart*. She considered it her floating kennel. As I gazed fondly across at her, she shook the white fringe out of her brown eyes and lifted her keen nose into the breeze. She had been my companion since puppyhood eight years previously, and we were devoted to each other. She greeted me ardently on my return from work; curled up in bed with me each night; insisted on healthy, daily activity; shared my meals; joined me in the shower; and was happiest when I mentioned the word "boat." We were off to see the world! Well, a small portion of it, anyway.

Sarah's notes on the pad of yellow-lined paper were crumpled history now, but they had provided a blueprint for my future. It had not proven easy to maintain the strategy and direction of my meeting with her. I eventually recovered from the unpleasant attack, but I found myself sinking all too easily back into the rut of comfort I had laboriously scooped out for myself over many years.

It hadn't been easy, not straightforward at all. It was all very well for Sarah to send me out of her office with a mandate, a decree, a reminder that my life nearly ended. I still faced the challenges of breaking free of the fond demands of a successful business, three grown children, dependent employees, and my comfortable condominium. It was like trying to escape from the embrace of an affectionate octopus. As fast as I successfully banished one clinging tentacle, another snaked up and entwined me from behind.

My mind split into the two familiar levels. One was telling me enthusiastically that I could do this. I could do whatever I wanted. I had the time, the money, and even the boat. There were no excuses. The other half of my brain, boringly prudent and cautious—Little Miss Ego—warned me not to toss away my mound of security quilts and risk my life in an unseemly quest. Risk my life? I nearly lost it!

Months and years started to slide past in trivial pursuits, but the signs kept intruding on my otherwise serene existence. I hadn't confessed to Sarah the truth of my lifelong cruising dream through the French canals to Greece. No, I'd abandoned that fantasy. Or had I?

I spotted an ad promoting New York State canals. They had canals in New York? I sent off for information. The fat folder of brochures which arrived astounded me. Okay, so it wasn't Europe, but there were Rome and Amsterdam, Athens and Berlin, Verona and Warsaw. With all those exotic destinations within sheltered canals so close to home, it sounded like my type of cruising.

I awoke next morning, my brain buzzing with a vivid dream. Greece, my long coveted destination, was closer than I thought. I ran downstairs in my pajamas and pulled out the U.S. atlas. Greece. Yes, there it was, right on the Erie Canal. I could do this! It was within my grasp. Fired with fresh enthusiasm, the plans began to click into place like Lego blocks from a toy box.

I arranged for a colleague to run my tour business for a season. *Dart* was strapped onto a borrowed trailer to be loaded on board a New York-bound freighter. A round of farewell parties sanctioned my plans. Friends and family gave me an enthusiastic send-off. Any last minute doubts I might have had were washed away by the enthusiastic and encouraging "Go for it, Mum," I heard repeatedly from my two daughters and son. "Have a great time, don't rush home, and don't worry about the money!"

*Dart* arrived in New Jersey aboard the Bermuda freighter *Oleander* and was launched in Liberty Landing Marina, right across from Manhattan and Ground Zero.

My long-vaunted, solo expedition was very nearly derailed, however, only days before the launch date. OK, I was nervous, twitchy, and anxious. I kept on reading and re-reading the guide books, unfolding and refolding the charts, listening to the weather forecast over and over again. I was doing just about anything to delay the final push-off. My cell phone rang.

"Björn? Hey!" It was my sailing buddy calling from Norway to announce his imminent arrival. "You're coming here, to New York, now?" I repeated in disbelief. What about my adventure, my challenge, my single-handed voyage? How would Björn fit into my plans, my boat, and my small space? On the other hand, I recalled his tall, rangy physique and thick gray hair that just begged to be rumpled. Maybe this would work out. It's only for a few days, I consoled myself. It was just a slight change in course, possibly even a sign. I met him at the airport in a rush of warm memories.

I'd met Björn the previous year when he sailed solo into Bermuda on his weather-beaten steel sloop *Nirvana*. During the months he awaited the installation of a new engine, we'd hung out companionably. I'd had a crush on him, but like so many world-sailors, he had a girl back home. I'd settled for being "best friends," and as such, we kept in touch by e-mail once he returned to Norway.

*Dart* awaited us at the New York marina. "She is so cute!" he enthused in his sexy, clipped Norwegian/Galveston accent. We unloaded a dozen plastic bags of supplies from the cab and headed down the ramp.

"Didi?" I turned to see who on earth Björn could possibly know at this marina. Incredibly, he had spotted an old girlfriend on the sailboat docked right across from *Dart*. Then to my horror, they sprang into each others arms. He flung her around in a whirl. I began to feel suspicious. What was going on here?

Didi and her companion Brian came aboard *Dart*. Both Brian and I watched resentfully as she and Björn renewed acquaintance. She showed him a scar on her leg, and from below in the cabin I saw him stroke it sympathetically. I ripped open packets of toilet rolls and flung them forcefully into a locker. So much for romance. It was an extraordinary coincidence to find Didi in the same marina, but perhaps it did serve to bump my emotions onto an even keel. It was a timely reminder that Björn had other women in his life, and, I had to admit, I had other men friends as well. A couple of hours later, *Dart* was loaded with supplies, and I, thankfully, headed north out of the marina while Didi waved frantically and Brian waved cheerfully.

Once under way, I relaxed enough to enjoy Björn's company. We quickly fell into our original camaraderie, and my companion soon displayed the eccentricities that had always endeared him to me.

It was May in New York. In some climes this means spring, but in New York it may just be a passing spring-like moment. "The sun's out! Let's get our clothes off!" Björn urged in true Scandinavian manner, still pallid from his protracted, northern winter. The thin, vernal sun glinted spectrally on his lanky frame and chalk-white skin as he wrenched a sweatshirt up over his head and settled back for a hopeful bask. A timely cloud briefly eliminated the feeble sunshine, and I had the perfect excuse.

"Björn, better get your clothes on, hmm? This is not Norway," I reminded him.

"Wretched uptight Americans," Björn grumbled as he struggled back into his tiny knickers teetering on one leg as the boat rocked and swayed. "They'd be having me in jail, I know."

Just an hour later, I had, in various layers, pulled on a tee shirt, a sweat shirt, a black nylon running jacket, my heavy fleece-lined winter jacket, and a full set of yellow waterproof foul-weather gear. I jammed on a brown woolly hat my Mum claimed to have knitted for me, wrapped a scarlet scarf round my neck, and pushed my freezing hands first into matching red woolen gloves, then blue ski gloves. Björn and Tucker had sensibly retired below and had the upturned terracotta flowerpot glowing on the propane stove.

*Dart* plowed her way through white-tipped waves, passing the stern cliffs of the Palisades, looking grim in the sudden overcast. The sky ahead was

*My chilled and frigid lips did their best to grin. "Life doesn't get much better than this!"*

ominously dark. Hailstones clattered on the deck, and I stood back in the cockpit to gain shelter under the small canvas bimini. The companionway stood open, and I could see that Björn was dozing. Tucker was tucked in beside him in the spacious red sleeping bag I had bought at the local thrift shop. I clutched the wooden, green-painted tiller and peered ahead through the gloom, looking for channel buoys and land marks. My chilled and frigid lips did their best to grin.

"Life doesn't get much better than this!" I thought.

"Shall I take a turn?" Björn called from the cozy cabin below.

"I'm fine," I called back. And I was. The river was deserted. We tied up at an isolated marina pier and spent a restless night alongside as the boat tossed and reared, jerking against her lines like a captured mustang.

We shopped, ate and drank too much, and slept well, he in the large scarlet sleeping bag, and I in my spacious vee berth up forward, buried under a mound of quilts. After a short visit to Troy, where we sampled the home brews at the famous dockside pub, it was time for the first lock.

"I have to learn to do this myself," I warned Björn. "You'd better let me handle the boat through the locks."

He agreed and sat quietly in the cockpit, puffing on his pipe and pretending to study charts, all the while keeping a wary eye on what I was up to. He muttered instructions out of the corner of his mouth.

"Slow now, out of gear, angle into the wall, reverse and stop the boat."

Too anxious, I would grab for the lock's attachment pipe while the boat was still moving ahead. *Dart* would keep going, her stern would swing out, and the bow pulpit would crash into the lock wall.

"You must stop the boat with the engine," Björn urged me.

As days progressed and we locked through time and again, I did learn to stop the boat. It surprised me that none of the lockkeepers gave Björn a funny look or a remark at his apparently chauvinistic idleness, leaving me to thrash about with lines and engine and tiller.

I had to learn fast, and soon locks no longer terrorized me, at least not until we motored into a particularly ancient lock on the Erie Canal. I gazed in horror at the soaring, dark, rough stone walls. There was no pipe or cable to tie to—just thick, filthy ropes suspended, swaying, from the dock way above.

"Help!" I appealed to Björn. "I don't think I can handle this one!"

He laid his pipe aside and stepped forward. Both of us grabbed a grubby, swinging line, one forward and one aft, and as the lock filled, *Dart* swung back and forth, pushed by the incoming flow of water. My confidence took a dive as deep as the lock. How could I do this alone? What if Björn hadn't been there? I was dry-mouthed and suddenly vulnerable and filled with horrid uncertainty.

# CHAPTER THREE

## Surviving the Rapids

It was Björn's idea to leave the buoyed channel near the next lock and be a little adventurous.

"Look," he said, puffing out a plume of Captain Black, his pipe stem stabbing at a point on the chart, "We can go 'round this little island and come out right near the lock."

*Here was a man who had sailed the Atlantic single-handed.*

I was reluctant, and as captain should probably have stood my ground, or rather my deck, and said no; but Björn's green eyes were gleaming at the prospect of adventure, and as he ran his fingers excitedly through his shock of graying hair, I could see he needed a diversion. After all, here was a man who had sailed the Atlantic single-handed to Bermuda where we met and became friends. Following channel markers up the river was hardly stimulating recreation.

We turned off to starboard, and, yes, it was quite lovely steaming down a tranquil, narrow, winding tributary of the Mohawk River. Vast chestnuts and delicate larches in spring green enlivened the river's edge, and small homes on the edge of the village revealed themselves in clearings. As we neared the end of the cut-off, I was disconcerted to hear a tumultuous roaring, roaring as in rapids, roaring as in millions of tons of water pouring, gushing, tumbling.

As we swung 'round the final bend, I saw with dismay that we were heading straight for a huge weir. The winter snow-melt and heavy spring rains had created an unusual amount of run-off that was now cascading over the dam and creating a turmoil of thrashing, foaming whirlpools and overfalls.

"Heavens, we have to steer though this to reach the lock," I thought nervously.

I glanced at the depth sounder and my scalp tingled, my stomach quaked, and my hand tightened on the wooden tiller. Five feet of water! Björn was always reminding me I only needed three feet six inches of water for *Dart* to creep through the shallows. But to me, where there's five feet, there's probably four feet just ahead and only three feet ahead of that.

I took a quick peek at the chart and was perturbed to see the little sharp, pointy, sketched triangles that indicated "rocks" just ahead. I looked up toward the lock, thankfully not far away now, and my eyes widened in horror. On the high, concrete wall next to the lock stood a line of men of various ages gazing fixedly in our direction. What were they expecting to see? Had they rushed here to watch some idiot try to shoot the rapids? Had the lockkeeper called out to passersby, "Hey, come and watch this idiot!"

I imagined *Dart* running aground in this chaos of turbulent water, her full keel snared on the jagged rocks, being pushed and rolled over, contents and crew swept away. I visualized Tucker paddling madly for shore, and Björn and I clinging to each other as my pink pajamas, collection of invaluable boating books, remnants of my precious Wayside china, brand new television, and bottles of Goslings Best Black Seal rum tumbled into the maelstrom, flung from a sinking, upturned boat.

We heaved and churned our way through the tumult of boiling, spume-flecked waves, the engine struggling as *Dart* hurled herself determinedly forward. The rapids reached out to snare my small craft, the torrents thundered, the air filled with spray, and huge dead tree branches and leaves raced past us in the seething current. Out of the corner of my eye, I anxiously watched as the depth sounder gradually flickered to six feet then to 10 feet.

Phew!

As we neared the tall, heavy, timber lock gates standing apart and offering a welcome open-armed sanctuary, I looked up at the row of watchers. Each held a long, slender fishing pole and gazed resolutely at the tip, waiting for the sign to reel in a plump fish.

They hadn't even noticed us.

*       *       *

When Björn left to fly home a few days later, I was left on my own. The confidence I had gained seemed to evaporate with him as he waved cheerfully and drove off in a taxi to catch the New York train.

"Come back! Stay!" I whispered to myself. I would never let him know that he was taking my assurance with him. I felt it escaping like effervescence from carelessly opened champagne. Immediate action was called for! I cast off the lines that tied me to the neighborly marina, checked the chart, and headed bravely for the next lock. Little Miss Ego was giving me grief as usual. "What are you whimpering about?" she chided. "You know how to handle a lock and a dock! Get on with it, you gormless lump!"

"Okay, okay," I replied, trying not to snivel.

I had thought I wanted my independence, my desired maverick life, but to my dismay, I found I didn't like being alone after all. A few hours of nervous solo motoring brought me to Rome, where I headed straight for the nearest phone.

*       *       *

I dropped the pay phone receiver back into its slot with a bang and roughly wiped a few stray tears off my cheek. The rain stuttered on the purple umbrella, and Tucker crouched on my feet in a vain attempt at shelter. My cell phone was out of range and useless, so I was forced to stand in the open, at the end of an unused warehouse on the town wharf. The conversation with my old friend Barrie had not gone well.

"Why can't you come and be with me now?" I begged him.

"What house guests?

"Who are they?

"Why can't you put them off?

"Are they more important to you than me?

"How can you tell me no and them yes?

"I need you here now.

"Not until August? In Montreal! That's the best you can do?" My phone card ticked off the minutes to England as I stood in a miserable drizzle near the public dock. Björn had only been gone a day, and it was enough to make me realize I couldn't continue the trip alone. I thought I had the stamina and the will, but they seemed to have dissolved.

Was my trip to end dismally in the rain in Rome? That sounded like a song, but I wasn't in a singing mood. No coins in a fountain for me here, just a dreary public park, dilapidated old warehouses, glowering clouds, and the distant glimmer of a fast-food sign.

I'd been on the phone for hours trying to find someone, anyone to join me on *Dart* to carry on. No luck. Friends and family were all gainfully employed or otherwise occupied. Only Barrie, retired and in England, would be free but not for weeks.

I would have to plough on manfully, or the female equivalent, bottom lip trembling, lump in throat, eyes fatefully brimming. Action proved the best remedy. I splashed back onto *Dart*, rubbed Tucker briskly with her green towel, and started a cleanup spree. Out went limp lettuce, questionable meat, damp cheese. Away went the large scarlet sleeping bag, firmly into deep storage; I needed no reminders of recent company. It was Tucker and I from now on—well, until August anyway.

It would be good to see Barrie, or would it? Faint tendrils of uncertainty snuck up behind me and tapped me lightly on the shoulder. A girlfriend had introduced us toward the end of his Bermuda contract some years previously, assuring me "Barrie has a sailboat, too. You'll have lots in common." I invited him for a sail in *Dart* and was amused to note how subtly he eased his way into the cockpit, slid his hand onto the tiller, gently removed the main sheet from my hand, and, before I realized it, wrested control from me and was sailing MY boat.

I shouldn't have been amused. I should have been warned. And now, had I done the right thing? In my quest for company, had I invited a serpent into my bilge? I had once told myself, "I never want to be on a boat with this man again."

"Oh, shoot," I thought distractedly, "that's pissed on the chips."

What would be worse, being joined by the man who drove me into months of expensive relationship counseling, or being alone? Then I recalled Björn's farewell remark to me, "Don't you go straight home, now." The cheeky bugger! Is that what he thought? That I'd give up the voyage and go home! I'll show him. There is no way I am quitting now, I told myself.

*I gazed appreciatively around the tiny cabin.*

I closed the companionway hatch and decided to make myself feel at home. I set the folding table with my colorful patchwork table mats, cutlery, and a wine glass. I heated up some delicious leftover spaghetti sauce and poured a glass of boxed cabernet. I gazed appreciatively around the tiny cabin. Soft lamplight gleamed on the brass ship's clock and barometer and on the varnished teak and cream paint. A band of decorative, embroidered trim bought many years previously, just after I acquired *Dart,* circled the cabin walls. Someone once said to me, "Y'know, this little boat is like a shawl. You can pull it around your shoulders for comfort." I felt that way on my first night alone and on many occasions during the two summers I voyaged with her. There were to be many evenings when after a day of wind and waves, docks and locks, when we were finally tied up and secure, and snug down below, I would pull her around me like a comforting, well-worn cloak and rest easy.

*I would pull her around me like a cloak.*

# CHAPTER FOUR

# Traveling Solo

The heavy iron doors thudded shut behind me, plunging me into gloom. Just inches from my face was a greenish-black, slimy stone wall, rough and pitted by years of wear. The grinding of heavy hinges jolted to a stop, leaving only the stealthy sound of dark water dripping. In front of me were a grimy, rusted ladder and two sturdy lengths of line holding me in position, one line to the stern of *Dart* and a second to her bow. I was now traveling solo on the Erie Canal.

I was pleased with myself as I made a perfect approach and entrance to the lock. As I picked out the ladder as my point of attachment and stopped right alongside, I mentally cheered to myself, "Yes!" As the sole occupant of the lock, I had been able to take my time and steer the tiny boat through the huge gates and between the vast towering walls. I mentored myself with a mantra, "Slowly now, out of gear, plenty of way on, good steerage, angle into the wall, not too close, into reverse and <u>stop</u> the <u>boat</u>." *Dart* obediently rested quietly and motionless alongside the lowest rungs of the 25-foot ladder. I left the tiller and stepped to her side where two lines lay ready to be looped over the ladder rungs.

A grinding, splashing noise warned of the sluices opening. The shadowy water billowed and rushed about within the lock, creating whirlpools and upwellings.

*Dart* is small and easy to hold in position, and I concentrated on moving the two loops of rope up the ladder rungs as we rose skyward. The incoming flow of water, piped through massive tubes on the floor of the lock, distributed the influx evenly throughout the lock.

The lockkeeper peered over the edge, and within minutes we were at ground level with a new view of the countryside. The water steadied and settled; the lockkeeper stopped by to check my registration and have a chat. I had paid for a season pass to all locks on the New York State Canal system, so he noted the serial number on the sticker.

"Bermuda, eh?" he commented. "I was there on the U.S. air base for a while. Great place!"

*I concentrated on moving the two loops of rope up the ladder.*

Pulling the dock lines into the boat, I eased the bow away from the lock side, took the tiller again, pushed the outboard engine into forward gear, and chuntered happily out of the lock. Ahead, the still, smooth water of the canal beckoned. Trees bent to the water's edge, early sunlight illuminated the golden fringe of rushes, and a light mist softened the scene. I leaned back to lift Wraith, my Raytheon auto helm, onto the tiller. She calmly took over the course, and I was free to rove about the boat, put the kettle on, check the chart for the position of the next marker, tidy up the dock lines, and just enjoy being in the moment.

Tucker, released from the cabin, jumped up and curled herself on top of the stowed folding bicycle in its bag, a cabin-top perch she preferred. She had learned a new command since we had been on board, "Go below," which she reluctantly obeyed when we approached a lock or dock. I kept a lookout for floating deadheads, lumps of driftwood, or sometimes an entire tree with only a blackened stump showing above water. Like an iceberg, much of their bulk was concealed, a menace to the unwary. The challenge ahead was Oneida Lake, my first lake. It was only 24 miles across, but a step outside the security of defined boundaries and a good practice run for dreaded Lake Ontario.

By afternoon I was ready to stop and regroup before heading across the lake. Referring to my chart books, I decided to spend the night at Sylvan Beach. Skinners Harbor Marina and Campground was a good choice. Tucker and I enjoyed the tranquil setting of mobile homes in a sheltered curve of the canal. A walk ashore revealed a seaside town, stalled in time, waiting for summer to arrive.

The marina owner's daughter Liz and her young, bearded friend Tom arrived by canoe and joined me for dinner on *Dart*. I listened, entranced by their tales of canoeing the Northern wilderness, portaging lightweight canoes at shoulder height.

The weather forecast for the next day was not good, but I reckoned that with an early start, I could beat the wind across the lake.

At dawn, I disconnected and coiled the power and dock lines. As we steamed out of the shelter of the canal, the view across the lake was grim. Grey clouds loomed menacingly, the wind was chill and brisk, and waves licked and splashed ominously at the end of the pier. Today was definitely not a day to cross the lake. I pushed the helm hard over; we returned to our sheltered berth and tied up again. I reconnected the power cable and the cable TV, made a cup of tea, popped the flowerpot on top of the propane stove to warm the snug cabin, turned on the television, and climbed back into bed. It was only 6:30 a.m.

By 10:30 a.m., a furious thunderstorm raged overhead, torrential rain streamed down, gusts of angry wind buffeted the treetops, and lightning glazed the heavy clouds. I made a mental note not to attempt to "beat the weather" in future.

The next day dawned peaceful and sunny, and after a successful crossing of Lake Oneida, I reached Brewerton where I found a group of cruising sailboats holed up waiting for locks to reopen. Both the Erie and Oswego Canals had been closed for two weeks due to high water levels and excessive floating debris caused by heavy rain further north. I was delighted to find company as I had been traveling solo for days. I had begun to wonder if I were the only sailboat heading north that year. The camaraderie of boaters was legendary, but I had yet to encounter it, and here, at last, was a timely opportunity.

There was no space for me alongside when I arrived at the public wharf, but I noted that the dog leg end of the dock appeared to be about 20-feet long with about four feet of water. It was just *Dart*'s size, and Tucker and I settled in contentedly. Parties broke out spontaneously day and night as we all nestled alongside. It was great to meet fellow cruisers and compare notes of recommended routes and potential hazards. I discovered that *Dart* was by far the smallest boat, and I gazed in amazement and admiration at the palatial floating homes with amenities some considered necessary—even essential.

*The dogleg end of the dock was just* Dart*'s size.*

On the other hand, the other boaters gazed with some astonishment at *Dart* and her solo skipper. Rob, owner of a huge schooner, chuckled as he showed us around his impressive vessel and confessed, "Marie likes a hot bath to start the day."

Tucker enjoyed playing football with the youngsters on the patch of grass alongside the dock while the adults chatted over snacks and cocktails. I met Eileen, whose condo looked across at the busy public dock. "The coffee pot is always on, so help yourself," she assured me as I plugged in my cell phone charger on her porch. "Do use the bathroom and laundry," she kindly urged me. I was glad to do so.

A couple of days later, good news was broadcast: The Oswego Canal was opened for those prepared to sign a waiver. I hadn't intended to take the Oswego Canal. My original plan was to head west on the Erie Canal, but it was fun to have the flexibility to change course and voyage with new friends. We all signed the waiver acknowledging that channel markers may have been swept out of position, and we were facing the danger of floating debris. We set off in convoy on a crisp, cold morning. It was only a day's voyage to reach Oswego. From there, the immense and intimidating reaches of Lake Ontario lay before us.

The other boats were heading in various directions, indifferent to the weather. They were larger and had crew. I moored in a small marina on the lake edge and wrestled with my fears. Suppose a huge storm blew up, catching us mid-lake? Suppose I fell overboard while Wraith was steering *Dart* and she arrived in Canada without me? What if the engine cut out, or I ran out of fuel? The list went on and on.

I listened compulsively, breathless and anxious, to the recorded messages of the weather service, huddled over the radio, hoping for good weather so I could leave, hoping for bad weather so I could stay. I told myself, "You can't get lost with your chart, compass, binoculars, depth-sounder, and GPS! I know that Lake Ontario has more shipwrecks than Bermuda, but, hey, you're in an ocean-going boat!"

I chatted with Cindy, the girl who manned the marina office, and she suggested a solution.

"If you need a crew" she said, "I'll come with you. I have to do a delivery to qualify for my captain's license."

Was this a sign? I decided it was, and with relief I accepted her offer. Even my children back home were glad to hear I would have company for the crossing. That was a surprise; I'd no idea they were concerned.

I waited patiently for a good weather forecast—southwest five knots—and Cindy arrived with her navigation kit and emergency rations of blueberry muffins. This is great, I thought, having a qualified captain along. Cindy plotted our chart position from the GPS, and we were apparently in the depths of the nearby hills. This was not a good start. I showed her how to plot and then felt a little more secure about my own ability.

I kept an eye on the GPS as the miles ticked off, and Cindy updated the paper chart every half hour or so, all the while munching on her huge bag of muffins and chattering ceaselessly. The lake was still and empty. I sent young Cindy below for a nap, and Tucker and I were able to leave Wraith in charge while we perched on the bow. The sound of the engine was left behind, and the bow wave chuckled merrily through the glass-smooth green water. With the binoculars, I was able to locate and identify the markers as they appeared gradually through the haze across the horizon.

The coast to the east was close enough to keep in sight, and gradually the mounds of the distant shore ahead rose grey and misty. Canada! We passed the halfway point, and I started to relax. This was really going well. I didn't feel scared any more. I hugged Tucker.

"We can do this," I told her. She dabbed a kiss on my nose.

A large sport cruiser raced past us throwing a massive wake that sent us heaving, bobbing, and cursing, and I called on the VHF radio to tick him off.

Ten hours after departing from Oswego, I flew my orange Q flag for customs clearance into Kingston, Ontario, Canada. The lake was behind me, and I felt buoyant and excited.

*I flew my orange Q flag for clearance into Canada.*

Cindy took the ferry home.

I proudly hoisted my Canadian flag to the masthead and swept up the muffin crumbs from the cockpit.

# CHAPTER FIVE

# The Movie in the Park

"Movie Night in the Park. Bring a friend and a blanket." That sounded fun. I was reading the notice board in the local public library. Strawberry festival at the church, antique sale in the market place, bagpipers parade on Sunday, and a craft fair in the park all weekend. It was all happening in Kingston, Ontario.

When I set off from New York and up the Hudson River with Björn, I felt I wanted to cover as much ground, or should I say water, as possible while he was with me. It meant more practice time for me at docking and locking, but once he left, I wanted to find somewhere to stop, to regroup, and to relax, somewhere I could call home for a while.

*The handsome limestone City Hall standing majestically in front of the marina in Kingston, Ontario.*

There were many small towns along the canal system that I motored into in happy anticipation, but I voyaged all the way to Canada before I found the right harbor to put down roots. I warmed to Kingston as soon as I steered into the marina at Confederation Basin and tied up *Dart* with relief after the 10-hour crossing from Oswego. It seemed a perfect setting. The handsome limestone City Hall stood majestically behind the grassy, flowered slopes of the waterfront park complete with fountain. My guidebook described it as "an excellent example of British Renaissance Tuscan Revival-style." As I stood at the crosswalk in front of the gracious civic edifice and gazed upwards, I nodded in agreement.

On my day of arrival, I was plunged straight into local culture with a display of bagpipe playing and Scottish dancing. The pipes I had learned to appreciate during the years my ex-husband, George, played in the Bermuda pipe band and practiced discreetly, heard but not seen, in the depths of the neighboring banana groves. The array of bands performing in Kingston was impressive, especially the tiny kilted tots who drummed and danced with gusto to exuberant applause.

It was Sunday, and I shortly discovered an antique fair and farmers market behind the vaunted City Hall. This was definitely my type of place and a relief not to have to motor, steer, navigate, dock, or lock for as many days as I chose. And now a movie in the park—what fun!

It was about a half-hour walk from the marina to MacDonald Park, passing the Marine Museum and moored icebreaker *Alexander Henry*, then along through the waterfront gardens and past the distinctive Murney Tower. Tucker and I were in good time and positioned ourselves comfortably on a park bench.

A youthful, diverse group was erecting a movie screen in the park gazebo and laying out rugs and folding chairs, ready for the showing. Two women joined me on the bench, and as often happens, one struck up a conversation with Tucker. We introduced ourselves, and I met Ann and Anne.

I couldn't remember the name of the group organizing the event. It was something neutral like Movie Buffs, and I hadn't quite figured out the connection among those in the assembling audience. Were they all walkers or joggers or library enthusiasts or company staff? There was something a little curious here, and I couldn't quite put my finger on it.

"What group arranged this movie showing?" I asked Ann.

"Gay Pride," she replied.

"Ah."

The sunlight dwindled, dusk crept negligibly across the lake toward us, and soon it was dark enough to begin the show. The movie proved dire; some ghastly teenage fantasy of bizarre, thwarted romance. I debated how I could make my departure without appearing prejudiced, chauvinistic, or just plain old-fashioned. A sudden rumble of thunder and the appearance of murky clouds impaled with lightning made the welcome decision for me.

"We'll continue the showing in the school hall," came the announcement.

"I'm heading back to the boat," I explained to Ann, "but I hope you can join me for tea tomorrow morning?" Tucker and I were drenched when we returned to *Dart* in the marina, but I was glad to be home to light the stove and warm us up.

The next morning, Ann arrived promptly, and after a mug of tea in *Dart*'s cockpit, we set off to tour the craft fair in the adjoining park. Ann, a talented and renowned local potter, was able to introduce me to many of the craftspeople she knew. We wandered the extensive grounds set up with myriad booths and tents and enjoyed with admiration the varied crafts of dozens of potters, weavers, carpenters, artists, photographers, and bakers. But first we established my criteria.

"Are you a lesbian?" she inquired politely.

"No," I asserted. "I just thought a movie in the park sounded fun."

\*                           \*                           \*

When Björn dubbed me a "tomboy," I was really proud. I stood a little straighter at the helm, stuffed my hands deep into denim pockets, and leaped off the boat onto the dock with a sprightly manner: a 60-year-old tomboy. Well, I always wanted to be a boy. Boys, I observed from a young age, had all the fun and all the freedom, and I did my best not only to keep up, but also to beat them at any pursuit.

When I was seven, I begged for a pair of grey flannel shorts, and then I couldn't be dragged out of them. The boys next door and I climbed trees, caught newts and sticklebacks in the local streams, stole birds' eggs, and rifled trash bins for our collections of cigarette packets, beer cans, and match boxes. We rented horses from the local stable. I rode Molly, a huge dapple grey. She kicked, so she had to wear a red ribbon on her tail to warn other riders to stay clear. I loved her anyway and learned to be wary of her hind quarters.

My brothers and I pedaled our sturdy, black, three-gear Raleigh bicycles for miles through rolling countryside and came home chilled and panting. If I couldn't be a boy, I'd act just like one. I slung on my gun belt, and the holsters sported two pearl handled Colts. My grandmother sewed me an authentic Indian costume complete with feathered headdress, and I switched readily from one side of the Wild West to the other.

*My grandmother sewed me an authentic Indian costume.*

*Swallows and Amazons* by J. Arthur Ransome introduced me to the adventures of the Walker children who seemed to have endless freedom and unlimited access to wonderful little sailboats, secluded islands, and sheltered lakes and rivers in the English countryside. Ransome helped to raise not one but many generations of boat-mad children, either living vicariously from the pages of his books or imitating them in reality.

I was one of them.

It was a good many years later that I read *Swallows and Amazons* to my 11-year-old son. We were spending a holiday on board *Dart* in the Chesapeake Bay shortly after I bought her, and I read him a chapter each evening.

I recalled reading about how the "Swallows and the Amazons" set off to launch their crafts, ready for another expedition. They had to stoop under boughs and step over brambles and push branches out of the way to find the two small sailboats drawn up on the beach. The *Amazon* was a fine little ship, with varnished pine planking, newer than the *Swallow*—of the same length, but not quite so roomy. The six youngsters and their adventures on the two famous boats enthralled readers for decades, including me.

Whenever I stood at *Dart's* helm, steered her into a sheltered cove, and tied up for a quiet night, I was really sailing with the Walker family, sailing with Arthur Ransome.

*         *         *

It was time to give *Dart* some attention. I'd been on the road almost continuously for weeks, and she was looking decidedly grubby and untidy. I liked the little mini-mast a friend had supplied to replace her proper mast, rigging and sails, all stored back in Bermuda, but she needed a rakish look. Yes, that was it, a touch of rake. I bought a six-inch bottle screw, shackled it onto the short forestay, and the little mast now leaned back with a rakish air. I gave it a coat of red enamel. Much better.

I pulled out my burgees and hauled them aloft, each sending a distinctive message: Seven Seas Cruising Association, Great Loop Cruisers Association, Women Aboard, Chesapeake Bay Schooner Race, and, of course, the Bermuda ensign. You just never know when a fellow member may pass by.

I hauled hanks of line, hose, a bilge pump, and a bucket of cleaning products out of the cockpit locker and replaced them neatly. It was a bit congested since I had, myself, installed an 11-gallon fuel tank. I was proud of the accomplishment, and the extra capacity was well worth the struggle.

I pulled up the teak cockpit grating, scrubbed it, then hosed off the cockpit floor. I plugged in the tiny vacuum cleaner and sucked up dog hair and dust from one end of Dart's small cabin to the other, shifting stacked books, baskets of groceries, dog toys, piles of charts, and cruising guides. I hauled the two large hampers out from the quarter berth and re-stowed the contents. Winter clothing and bedding and the electric heater went away, and out came summer cottons, cabin fans, bathing suit, and beach towels.

I polished up the propane stove and stainless steel sink, and emptied and scrubbed the ice box. The clothing locker over the vee berth was emptied, and garments folded neatly and replaced. Woodwork was polished, fiberglass buffed, and brass shined. I lifted the cover off the outboard engine and checked the oil, then tilted the engine up and scrubbed off the propeller. Wraith, my Raytheon auto-helm, was disconnected, wrapped in a tee shirt, and laid gently to rest in the clothing locker until needed.

Two open shelves on either side of the cabin were a bit useless, as anything loose would slide off or fall over, so I bought square wicker baskets to fit on the shelves. These held groceries, bottles, magazines, books, and dog toys. The television fit neatly onto the widest part of the shelf.

I had screens with lead weights that held themselves in place over the fore hatch and the main companionway. I handled them carefully as they were made by the original owner's wife over 20 years earlier. I thought of her every time I used the screens. She died of cancer, still bravely cruising with her husband in their Hans Christian 33.

*Dart's* exterior needed some attention, too, so I hosed her off, then started polishing the cabin sides with rubbing compound and wax. She soon gleamed in the early summer sun and was finally looking ship-shape and admirable. I was content that she was spick-and-span at last. There hadn't been time or opportunity during the voyage north, and I had been conscious of a gradual build-up of grunge within and without.

I was aware, too, in the marina of the constant washing and polishing of boats all around me. Once I joined in, I felt part of the scene. Boaters stopped by with advice and remarks. Dock neighbor Conrad had been meticulously buffing his sleek gold and purple "cigarette" boat, and he kindly advised the best brand of wax. He and his companion dressed in purple, their towels drying on the dock were purple, and even their dock lines were purple.

*Dart's* cream hull was smartly offset with her dark green canopy and green painted railings and wood trim. I'd long since given up on varnishing and painted all the teak dark green.

I trotted up to the local ship's store and bought a pair of handsome green nylon dock lines, dug out a green tee shirt, smoothed it out, put it on, poured myself a Goslings Bermuda Black Seal rum and Coke, and sat back, finally feeling part of the Kingston boating scene.

*Feeling part of the Kingston boating scene.*

# CHAPTER SIX

# A Mysterious Visitor

It was a hushed night docked at secluded little Cedar Island—just the occasional call of a night bird and watery plop from some shore creature enjoying a moonlight dip. Tucker and I were snug below when the patter of footsteps and rattling of claws on the deck above woke me.

"What on earth is Tucker doing on top of the boat?" I thought to myself sleepily. But Tucker was beside me fast asleep. Who, or what, with sharp claws was walking casually about the boat? The half moon yielded enough light to illuminate the cockpit beyond the screen over the companionway. I was startled to see a small face peering in, with two pointed ears and a round furry head silhouetted. Tucker saw the image at the same instant, exploded into action, dove through the screen, leapt off the boat, and went racing up the steep, rocky path beyond the dock.

There was no point calling her, and I certainly wasn't about to go stumbling around in the dark at that time of night to find her. I lay expectantly and waited. Twenty minutes later, I heard a series of barks from across the cove. I peered out of the boat and saw she had given up the chase and was now across on the far dock, barking at muskrats and probably about to wake the boat campers slumbering there. Cursing furiously, I grabbed a flashlight, collar, and lead and floundered up the sheer cliff path, around the cove, and down the far side. I gripped Tucker and dragged her angrily back with me by the scruff of her neck, berating her, as far as one can berate in a whisper. I flung her into her bed and locked up the boat.

In the morning, I apologized to my neighbors, who looked amazed and assured me they hadn't heard a thing. As regards to my visitor, they reckoned it must have been a raccoon. I was still mad at Tucker which was a bit pointless. She had no idea why I was cross. She was a hunter and had only been following her instinct. I guess I shouldn't have bought a terrier. I really wanted a dog who would curl up on my knee in the evening and be obedient and pliable. Well, I consoled myself, all relationships between dogs and man are a compromise. Maybe Tucker would have liked to live in the hills of

England with a pack of fox hounds where she could hunt every day. Perhaps I was her compromise. I gave her a long, loving hug.

\*        \*        \*

*My friends Ken and Rosemary had introduced me to Cedar Island.*

My friends, Ken and Rosemary, had introduced me to Cedar Island. We were dock neighbors in Kingston Marina and owned, so we believed, the two cutest boats there. Ken and Rosemary were tying up their Nonesuch 22, *Mini,* when I stopped by to admire their neat little craft one day and was offered a guided tour. Rosemary fired up the stove in their petite galley, brewed a pot of smoky Earl Grey tea, and we relaxed in the cockpit. I learned that they owned a condo overlooking the marina in Kingston.

"When we bought it, we never really thought we'd retire to live here," they told me. "But it suits us very well." Ken and Rosemary had emigrated to Canada from England some 35 years previously, raised their family in Canada, and were now visited regularly by a veritable squadron of grandchildren who piled onto *Mini* for daily excursions every summer. On my way back from the farmers' market, I pressed upon them part of a large bagful of tomatoes, sure that I could never eat so many before they over-ripened.

A couple of days later I returned to *Dart* from the laundromat and found a note inviting me for a cruise on *Mini*. There was a light breeze on the harbor that day, and *Mini* sailed us quietly along the coast. The breeze died, the little diesel engine was started, and we docked at nearby tiny Cedar Island for afternoon tea. It was a fortuitous introduction to Parks Canada's wonderful array of public facilities in the Thousand Islands. Maintained by the government, each island provided campers and boaters with dock space, picnic tables, barbecues, a rustic dry toilet, pathways, and camp grounds. Payment was modest and based on the honor system. The mailboxes were emptied regularly by the patrolling staff.

I determined that should I feel brave enough, Cedar Island would be on my list of destinations. Just a few days later I courageously set out on *Dart* to see if by chance there was dock room on the island. It was only two days after Canada Day, so I felt fortunate to find space. I tied up easily with some assistance from those already docked.

Within minutes, Graham arrived on the dock next to *Dart* and introduced himself.

"This is a Flicka, isn't it?" he inquired enthusiastically. "I've always admired the Flicka and wanted to see one," he said as I invited him onboard.

He and his wife, Felicity, were on the adjoining dock on their lovely little Bluejacket 23, *Cockleshell*, a Garden-designed sloop, also without mast and sail rig, I was pleased to note. At least I wouldn't be the only mast-less sailboat in the cove. I did a quick survey of my food lockers and figured I had enough ice, food, and wine to stay for three days, so I settled in. Once the day visitors departed, I pulled *Dart* across to share dock space with *Cockleshell,* and we spent a relaxing weekend swimming, reading, and visiting back and forth on the two kindred boats, comparing notes on voyages past and future.

The bay was sheltered and peaceful. A light breeze soughed through the pine trees above us; small waves lapped delicately on the encircling rocks but barely moved the boats. The paddlewheel tour boats passed on a regular schedule, pointing us out to intrigued sightseers, cameras aimed. I wondered if the passengers envied us—the pair of diminutive, classic, cream-colored boats neatly moored alongside an enchanting island.

Tucker and I swam together across a small pool near the dock to a rocky point that jutted out into the river. I don't think I had ever swum in water so cold, but it was refreshing; at least I kept telling myself that! It was certainly delightful to haul out of the crisp, fresh water onto a smooth, granite boulder to warm up and dry off in the sunshine.

*A pair of diminutive, classic, cream-colored boats neatly moored alongside an enchanting island:*
Dart *and* Cockleshell.

Tucker shook herself vigorously, then took up her accustomed stance, peering deeply into the clear water, looking for fish. Ever the hunter, fish had recently taken the place of four-legged or feathered prey, thank heaven. I'd had to accept the fact that I was living with a serial killer.

She has such a cute, fluffy, innocent little face with an engaging expression and such demure brown eyes. But her true nature is ruthless and heartless, especially when it comes to chickens and ground hogs.

I met her when she was a week old. I have a photograph of me holding a little white mite in my hand, only about five inches long and eyes tightly shut. Actually, that's not quite true. The pup I was holding was the one I picked out of the litter, but it wasn't Tucker.

Tucker's mum impressed me as a gracious, mannerly dog. She calmly sat beside me, stretched out her head, and touched my nose with hers. When I found out her name was Jill, I felt this was an auspicious sign. I grinned up at my girlfriend, Barbara, who was recording the encounter with my camera.

Tucker's dad, Jack, a mostly white, rough-coated terrier, was in a nearby pen and sat with his back turned, eyeing us occasionally over his shoulder.

*I met her when she was a week old.*

Two weeks later, I drove back to the owner's property only to find the pup I had chosen had a smooth coat. Meanwhile, the real, the eventual, rough-coated Tucker already had a fuzzy little face and was filled with energy and adventure and gleaming, brown, mischievous eyes.

Tucker was officially chosen and named. Three weeks later, I picked her up and brought her home. The dog-raising books suggested a box beside the bed for sleeping pups. Tucker would have none of it! She squeaked and fussed so piteously from her box that I relented and brought her into my bed. She snuffled and nosed about and settled down happily in my hair.

*Beef rib bones were a favorite.*

I bought a woven basket and carried her with me everywhere, slung over my shoulder. Her bed was cluttered with toys. Beef rib bones were a favorite, and soon her basket was rattling like a mummy's tomb. I didn't like living with a killer, but killer she soon proved to be. Chickens were a favorite prey of hers. Over the years, I reimbursed enough chicken owners to start my own branch of Kentucky Fried.

She was only a year old and with me at the boatyard, playing happily and sniffing out rats along the water's edge among the many boats and under piles of discarded lumber and rigging. Busy working on *Dart*, it was a while before I realized she had vanished. Calling and whistling brought no response. I climbed anxiously into the car and started driving through the neighborhood. Down a nearby driveway, in a neighbor's yard, I came across a pen of young pullets, all dead. Tucker was in the wire pen with them, her mouth full of feathers, and the cage full of feathers and nine dead chickens. She looked quite pleased with herself until she saw my face; then her expression faltered. Forcing my way into the pen, I gripped her, flung her into the car, and looked at the destruction around me.

I thought to myself, I can tiptoe away or I can write a note for the owners. I only considered Plan A for a split second and then pulled out a notebook and started a note of apology. It was just as well. A car pulled in behind me, and the family—parents and two young boys—piled out, looking in dismay at the drift of feathers and scattered limp bodies. I started to apologize profusely.

"Oh, we're just house sitting," they said. "They're not our chickens. You can deal with the owners when they get back, or they can deal with you." A check for $50 later settled the matter, though not very amicably.

# CHAPTER SEVEN

# A Thousand Islands

Doug, a fellow solo-cruiser, had gone into a huddle with Richard and Julya while leaning over the navigation table in their spacious and comfortable trawler-yacht docked near *Dart*. All eyes were on a chart of the Thousand Islands in the St. Lawrence River. I peered over a shoulder and mentally reeled back in horror. The page they were studying showed at least a thousand small islands all jammed together with barely a passageway between them. The entire page of the chart book was a confusion of minuscule isles and islets.

No wonder Richard and Julya were taking advantage of Doug's local knowledge. A stranger would surely soon be hopelessly lost and probably disappear for months within the mayhem of markers, buoys, lights, and beacons. Doug, on the other hand, had lived in the area for years while married. Since his divorce, he moved aboard his Hallberg Rassy sailboat and was now securely anchored within a veritable network of islands.

"No way will I ever go there," I declared to myself stoutly, appalled at the incredible dangers that obviously lurked in such confined quarters.

They muttered away to each other about the "navy islands," the "fleet islands," the "admiralty islands." The very names reeked with experienced seamanship that would surely be way beyond my capabilities. No doubt the admiral could find his way about, not to mention the navy or the entire fleet, but me? It was doubtful.

As I glanced at the chart, my stomach rumbled with anxiety. I could just imagine myself losing track of the safe course, suddenly finding myself surrounded by nasty little identical rocky islands. Where would the shallows be, the reefs, the single, pointy boulder lurking just out of sight, right below the surface, right in front of *Dart* as I steamed unwittingly along? Would islanders and picnickers all be watching as I ran humiliatingly aground? Would they jeer and shout or rescue me? Ah, but how time allays the worst of imaginary fears and lulls the most tremulous of mariners into just one short voyage into the unknown.

It was only a few weeks later that I found myself untying *Dart* from Kingston's congenial city marina and setting off for Gananoque, a 21-mile voyage into the wilderness of the Thousand Islands. I untied the boat, but that was almost as far as I got. There was a stiff breeze blowing into the marina which made it difficult—dangerous even—to attempt to maneuver *Dart* under power. The sensible course would have been to walk her right around at her pier so she was facing outwards and ready to motor straight out of the marina. She is so easy to turn using long lines and a strategic fender or two.

For some reason, I decided to back out under power and turn the rudder to steer outwards. That just didn't work. As soon as the wind caught her bluff bow, she was blown in quite the wrong direction. Power applied to the motor merely compounded the problem as prop-walk dragged her stern round until we were now facing and being blown downwind right into the busy marina. As I wrestled with the revving engine, clashing gears, and wayward tiller, I noted with wry amusement that boat owners nearby were running hastily toward their moored craft, preparing to fend off a very small boat apparently run amok and obviously out of control.

Eventually, I gave up all hope of exiting the marina and backed clumsily into an empty bay. A courteous boat-owner came to help, and I asked him to take my bow line and hold onto it while I maneuvered around the end of the pier until Dart was facing *out* of the marina. This he obligingly did, and I finally set off somewhat abashed and even more insecure about the network of channels I had ahead of me.

As it often turns out, I did all the worrying well in advance. The voyage went smoothly, and as I breathed in the cool air that stroked calming fingers through my hair, I relaxed and shook the tension from my shoulders. "This is the life," I thought to myself as the feelings of stress turned gradually into the pleasure of the moment and a feeling of accomplishment and capability.

I carefully followed the Bateau channel passing Cedar Island, Milton Island, and Treasure Island. Wolfe Island was south of me, providing a nice lee from the fresh breeze. I gave the huge Wolfe Island ferry a wide berth as they made their regular crossing. I had taken the ferry from Kingston over to Wolfe Island just recently and stocked up at the famous bakery there: garlic bread, iced buns, and such huge delicious currant-filled butter tarts that I had to ration myself to one daily.

I passed Gillespie Point and watched the markers carefully for the dog leg past Beaurivage Island and then to Spectacle Rocks. The river sparkled in the noonday sunshine, and the viridian pine trees were a fine counterpoint to the dark, rugged rocks and smooth, pink, granite islands. "Gan" marina was soon in sight, and on the VHF radio the dockmaster told me to pick any available dock. I selected an easy one close at hand and made a four-point perfect landing, giving myself full marks. I'd made it into the Thousand Islands! I could rank myself alongside the "admiral," the "navy," and even the "fleet."

*The river sparkled in the noonday sun.*

*I made a perfect landing in Gananoque.*

# CHAPTER EIGHT

## Night on the Cataraqui

I met Donna on the Cataraqui River, or should I say "in" the Cataraqui River, when she swam across the river to meet me one evening.

It had been a long day. I left Kingston one morning in early July and plunged straight into the Cataraqui River. A flight of four locks at Kingston Mills lifted us some 60 feet into Colonel By Lake and then into the River Styx where the charts warned of "stumps and deadheads" on both sides of the channel. I kept a wary eye on the buoys and channel markers as the river wound through delightful countryside and I felt as if I were sailing through Sussex County in pastoral England. We passed cornucopian fields, rustic barns and gleaming aluminum silos, herds of relaxed cows, sun-bleached

*The river wound through delightful countryside.*

fences, and diminutive waterside cottages. I had planned to spend the night on the dock wall at Upper Brewers lock, but on exiting the lock, I saw at once that the wharf was jammed with moored craft of varying sizes. Disappointed, I steamed on, but a glance at the chart showed that Jones Falls was an additional two hours away through Cranberry and Whitefish Lakes.

I was already tired from the anxiety of untying myself (and *Dart*) from the comfortable docks of Kingston Marina, as well as the stress of negotiating several locks, as I commenced the voyage into the Rideau Waterway. It had been a day of "lake anxiety" and a touch of "dock 'n' lock fright." The prospect of un-knotting *Dart*'s dock lines and pushing her, once again, away from the security of a comfortable marina created huge trepidation. Will the engine start? Will the weather change? Will I find my way? I became compulsive and twitchy, couldn't eat, dashed back to the marina toilet, and stowed and tidied below until I couldn't postpone any longer the inevitable departure.

Getting underway came as a huge relief. It was a delight: the breeze through my hair, the patterns of sunlight across the river surface as clouds drifted by, the silhouetted islands, and the familiar red and green markers that thankfully matched those on my chart. The landscape became residential. Steep banks clothed in trees in full summer leaf rose on both sides of the river, and waterside homes proliferated. Families were enjoying the early evening sun, children swimming and jumping off docks and piers; the waft of barbecue smoke and the echo of merry voices filled the air.

Searching for a potential spot for the night, I passed what seemed to be the only unoccupied dock in the area. Steps lead from the small wooden jetty up a sheer, rocky pathway to a timber house on the hillside. I wondered if I might tie up there.

I motored past a large family group on the opposite bank who waved cheerfully and called out a friendly greeting. Making a quick decision, I pushed the tiller over and turned *Dart* around. I called up to the family party, "Do you think the owners of the dock across the river would mind if I tied up for the night?"

"No, they wouldn't mind at all," came the cordial response. "It's our dock, and we're over here house-sitting. Make yourself at home."

With great relief, I steered *Dart* across the river and swiftly tied up to the small but sturdy plank dock. Minutes later both Tucker and I were overboard and cooling off in the fresh river water. I opened a bottle of chardonnay and cooked boiled eggs while the fresh asparagus from Kingston's farmers' market steamed over the same pot. At dusk I noted a figure swimming across the river. Donna, shaking off her damp, blonde hair, climbed up the wooden dock ladder and came over to *Dart* for a visit.

"You're more than welcome to stay for the weekend," she assured me. "We're just across the way looking after a neighbor's house, and that's my father-in-law next door." She showed me where to plug into a power outlet, but I didn't need power that night.

The moon gleamed on the mellow water, and small creatures splashed and squeaked on the fringe of the river. A few dainty bats darted after twilight insects. The sounds of festive parties dwindled away, and a tranquil hush lay over the Cataraqui River. I looked over at Tucker curled into a furry ball, content after a cooling swim and a tasty dinner and now quite relaxed in

*I swiftly tied up to Donna's small but sturdy dock on the Cataraqui River.*

her home and with the companion she loved. I chuckled at myself, applying my feelings to Tucker. Yes, I, too, was in the boat I loved, happy with the company, far from home and yet at home. *Dart* hung suspended in the still river, secured to a secluded dock yet ready at the turn of a key to move forward into new adventures. The memory of this peaceful evening would long remain a favorite, one that I would often recall and feel the gathering of tears of reminiscence.

# CHAPTER NINE

# The Long Drop

I lost my nerve in Smiths Falls. I can't think why. I'd had a very pleasant time in this modest and agreeable town.

I'd emerged from the last lock of the day into the basin near the town. I steamed slowly past the municipal marina and noted that each of the finger piers was occupied. Docking was permitted on the rails alongside the local park, but this area was full too. Across the pool I spotted a small space between two moored craft and a friendly figure waving enthusiastically. I motored across, eyed the gap, and figured I could just squeeze in with some help. The help was standing right alongside the dock, waiting patiently to take my lines. A few minutes of maneuvering, and I was tied up. I recognized my helper as the father of a group of youngsters on board the homely steel tugboat *Audacity*. I had helped them tie up in Westport a few days earlier—not that they needed help with all those teenagers on board, but it seemed the neighborly thing to do. I knew I could dock myself, but it was still comforting to see someone step forward and be on hand to grab a line.

Tucker and I were now securely alongside a delightful park with paddling pool, flower beds, and shade trees, and only a short walk to the nearby shops. There was no shore power, but I had enough battery power for 24 hours and sufficient ice to keep the groceries cool. Moored just ahead of us was a handsome little traditional motor vessel, a kind of mini-trawler. It had an English look to it, too, reminiscent of a Maurice Griffith. I surreptitiously examined it. It was a Maple Bay 27. What a nice little boat, I thought, that would suit me very well—I mean, if I should ever want a bigger boat...not really...I loved *Dart*.

Tucker and I set off for our usual exploratory walk of the neighborhood. I needed a haircut. Not far from the marina, I spotted an intriguing offering "Antiques, and Trims." I tied Tucker up outside and stepped into a delightful antique shop with the traditional collection of gleaming old mahogany furnishings topped with Victoriana: brass lamps, china figurines, leather-bound books, gleaming silver, and copper. I could hear a lively conversation from behind an ornate Chinese lacquer screen. I peeped round and saw the salon, a simple arrangement of salon chair, sink, and a lovely antique mirror. A client was having her hair set in curlers while the hairdresser kept up a cheerful conversation. I made an appointment to return shortly. Soon it was my turn to enjoy the antique dealer's skill with scissors.

"I love it here," she told me as she snipped away. "I've always wanted an antique shop, but I've been a hairdresser forever. We live out in the country, and I had an hour commute everyday to the beauty shop where I worked. When my husband had a heart attack and quit work to stay home, I decided to make a change. I found this shop and loved it. But my hairdressing clients were so upset that I thought, well, maybe I can combine the two. So here I am now in my own place, the best of both worlds. My husband and I go out in the car weekends, buying for the shop, and my hairdressing clients are happy too." As I walked away with the breeze cooling my newly exposed ears, I thought how pleasant to find a truly contented person.

That afternoon I was puttering about below decks when I heard the chirping of young voices. "Look at the baby boat, Mummy and Daddy, look at the baby boat!" Since my family had long ago nicknamed *Dart* "baby boat," I was intrigued to meet her new fans.

*Dart was nicknamed "Baby Boat."*

Three little girls were perched like sparrows on the waterside railings gazing at *Dart*. I invited them aboard. "Can we, Mummy and Daddy? Please!" they begged their parents. They clambered happily aboard, and I showed them the little stove, the small sink, the ingenious ice box, the tiny TV. They were entranced, and I could see they felt they were in a unique floating play house. They really didn't want to leave. I pulled out the bag of Bermuda lapel pins for them to choose. This proved so difficult, I added, "Well, take one each for your best friends as well."

The choices made, they climbed reluctantly off the boat. About 10 minutes later they were back with "Mummy and Daddy" for a photo of *Dart,* her skipper, and the ship's dog.

Next morning, I mounted an expedition to the grocery store for food, ice blocks, and water, and I should have been ready to set off again. So why did I feel shaky and nervous all of a sudden? Was it because I had peered deep into the next lock? The water was down and a fellow-boater had remarked that it must be all of a 60 foot drop. Maybe it was a hormonal drop—all of 60 feet.

Why feel so anxious now? I'd been doing so well, docking with aplomb and skill, finding my twisting route through the network of waterways, getting myself in and out of dock space, riding the lock waters up and down. Was it the wine last night...or too much caffeine this morning?

So it was with some trepidation, shaky hands, and queasy stomach that I started the engine, cast *Dart* loose, and motored across to tie up on the blue line to await passage through the lock. I figured it was like falling off a horse—which I did many times in my youth. It's always best to climb back on and gallop off again. So off I galloped. I didn't do too well at first. As the green light flashed on and I prepared to steer into the lock, I didn't push the bow out far enough and the fenders hitched up onto the dockside and brought her to an awkward stop. I jumped off, gave her bow a good shove and set off again, more successfully. As the day proceeded, the jittery feelings receded, the hormones balanced, and the nerves were soon relegated to the past.

# CHAPTER TEN

# The Ice Man Cometh

*Dart*'s cockpit was littered with the dead bodies of dreaded deer flies. I hadn't known what they were on the first day they made their move, and merely brushed the strange little grey and white concord-shaped flies off my legs. That was a big mistake. Two days later, each bite was glowing hotly and sending me into a maniacal frenzy of itching and scratching. Insect bite sprays helped, but at night it took a dose of two antihistamines to help me sleep.

Today, I was ready for them. I had on long cotton pants and a man's white shirt with long sleeves and upturned collar. I recognized that when the boat was within a quarter mile of the bank, these vicious wolves on wings made their appearance. I now wielded a sturdy fly swatter, and few flies broke through my cordon of defense. I noticed they preferred to make the initial landing on something black and shiny. The bulkhead compass and the black nylon bag containing my folded bike were two favorites. As soon as I spotted the first dive, the swatter fell and pulverized the small bodies. It was challenging at times to steer a safe course, tiller in one hand, swatter in the other, one eye out for channel markers, and the other out for deer flies.

The Ottawa River stretched ahead of me, broad, smooth, and shallow with the distant Laurentian hills piled up against the clouds on my left while on my right, houses, lawns, and shade trees—maples and willows—massed on the river's edge. We had been gradually entering an extensive housing district, and the banks were highlighted with a variety of homes from rustic log cabins to sprawling ranch houses to Tudor mansions complete with black and white timber trim and diamond-paned windows.

Ahead, I noticed a small, strange craft scurry out from the southern bank and head straight across the river. It seemed to have originated in a residential neighborhood and had sped across to a park area where families had gathered to enjoy an afternoon swim on a shallow, sandy shoal. Could it be a local ferry service, I wondered?

*I saw a blue and white pontoon boat. Ice cream!*

When it reappeared, I focused the binoculars and saw a blue and white pontoon boat festooned with bunting and sporting a colorful fringe around the canopy. As we pulled closer to the boat, I noted writing on the side of the frame: ICE CREAM. "Ice cream," I called down to Tucker who was dozing in the cabin below. At the sound of her favorite treat, she sprang aloft with enthusiasm, her hair mussed and ears sleep-crushed.

As we watched, a small speedboat stopped beside the pontoons, and the family on board made their purchases. Then it was our turn. We maneuvered alongside, and the proprietor and I both put our engines into neutral and drifted with the current for a few minutes, linked together with a couple of lines from boat to boat. I requested a strawberry cone and a cup of vanilla for Tucker. She was perched with me in the cockpit, looking very expectant, having shaken herself thoroughly in preparation. Clad in his blue-and-white-striped uniform with smart white apron and hat, our marine ice cream-man handed over our requests in exchange for a couple of dollars. As we bid a cheerful farewell, I was far enough away from the banks to forget about deer flies for a while.

I laid down the fly swatter and enjoyed the delicious cool refreshment as we carried on our voyage to Ottawa. Tucker slurped happily, head down in her cup and tongue licking every last delicious morsel. I recalled as we carried on along the gentle curves of the broad, shallow river that I was retracing the steps of the old-time fur trappers who used this same route to travel north in spring and south in the fall with their valuable cargoes of pelts, furs, and hides (beaver, seal, and mink) for shipment to Europe to grace the heads and shoulders of the aristocracy.

I doubt they ever came across an ice-cream man.

# CHAPTER ELEVEN

# The Flight of Eight

*Dart* swung 'round a wide bend, and I was startled to see a really low bridge dead ahead. I yanked the engine out of gear and ticked myself off for not paying attention. *Dart* idled in the slight current as I thrashed around in the cabin, pulling out the charts. Ah, Pretoria Bridge—with a 10-foot clearance when closed—which it obviously was. Not to worry. I untied the two shrouds that held up *Dart*'s red mini-mast, lowered it forward to rest on the lifelines, and we carried on. As we motored forward, the owner of a passing cabin cruiser called out to me, "The bridge will open for you if you wait."

"I'm all set, thanks," I called back, and we dove into the gloom beneath.

Ottawa! At last. I could hardly believe that my little boat and I were steaming into the heart of the capital of Canada. It was a thrilling moment.

The day began with a straightforward run through Dows Lake and eight locks, then the final five-mile canal approach within city limits. On both banks the city's waterside trail was thronged with walkers, joggers, cyclists, and roller-bladers. Buildings increased in size as we neared the civic center. I knew we were approaching the tie-up area, so I motored forward at a circumspect speed, paying closer attention to the chart, now on the seat beside me. With the binoculars I could see that the public dock looked pretty jammed up so we ducked into the first small space we spotted and tied up just beyond the Mackenzie King Bridge.

Tied up in Ottawa! I was so excited I couldn't wait to get ashore and just walk about.

The air hummed with the sounds of the Jazz Festival already underway, and the city churned with an amicable throng of casually dressed music-lovers. I could hear at least two bands playing in nearby parks, and the air reverberated with contrasting rhythms. Tucker and I followed the flow of the crowd to the nearby arena where we sat at the top of a tall flight of steps to enjoy the boisterous concert underway. We munched a burger each, mine washed down with a beer as a special treat. Then, of course, I had to head back to *Dart* for a nap.

*Tied up in Ottawa! I was so excited.*

The evening provided *Son et Lumiere* at Parliament House. It was a magical event on the grounds of the handsome parliament buildings with slides and movies depicting the history of Ottawa and the settling of Canada projected right onto the exterior walls. I was so carried away, I promised myself if they sang "Oh, Canada," I would want to become a Canadian. We did sing it, of course, and I joined in wholeheartedly. I have to admit that

Canadians I spoke with warned me I'd better spend a winter here before I think any more about staying permanently.

The next morning Tucker and I set out early to collect coffee, apple fritters, and papers and to find a restroom. Later, as I tidied up the boat, I heard a marching brass band playing and recalled the Changing of Guard ceremony. Tucker and I dashed up to the Parliament Building and found a place along the rope perimeter just in time. The smart, scarlet-uniformed guard performed admirably, and even Tucker was entranced. In fact, so

*The guard performed admirably, and even Tucker was entranced.*

entranced was she that many of the visitors around us were equally entranced watching Tucker being entranced.

It was so comical to see this little white, woolly dog gazing, apparently enthralled, at a military ceremony. On the way back to the boat, we both peered over the Wellington Street Bridge and the impressive flight of eight locks way below. "We can do that," I assured Tucker. She looked dubious.

*We peered over the Wellington Street Bridge at the impressive flight of eight locks way below.*

At Byward Market, I stocked up on salads, veggies, fruit, hot roasted chicken, and fresh-baked garlic bread, and by 2:30, *Dart* was parked at the top of the flight of eight locks. So many boats were being locked upwards that it was 7:00 p.m. before *Dart* and the only other downward boat were called in for the 80-foot descent. We entered each lock at ground level, and young lock hands in their smart green shirts were nearby to help with lines. It was all very smooth and proficient. The lock master controlled the proceedings much like an orchestral conductor, with arm and hand signals to his youthful and enthusiastic team. Each lock needed to be opened and closed in unison, and the flight was negotiated with professional ease.

By the time I motored out onto the Ottawa River and across to the Hull Yacht Club, I was pooped. But I had time to gaze backwards and admire the striking view of the south side of the Parliament Buildings with the stunning flying buttresses and the copper rooftops echoing those of the castle-like Chateau Laurier across the waterway. I tied up at Hull Yacht Club Marina where Patrick, a fellow-boater I met in Smiths Falls, had promised a reservation for me. Nicole introduced herself from a nearby cabin cruiser.

"You are on your own!" she exclaimed in amazement in her delightful French accent. "You are so brave—but don't you get lonely?"

I thought about that over the next couple of hours. Was I lonely? I wasn't aware of being so. It was just the two of us on *Dart*, but we were surrounded by the amenable company of fellow boaters. Okay, there were evenings when I admitted to myself that it would be nice to share a glass of wine in the cockpit with an amicable companion. In fact, I thought I might, perchance, find one. I didn't feel it my karma to remain single—surely this was a temporary state? But it was necessary at this point in my life to rebuild a distinct loss of confidence. This voyage was something I needed to achieve alone.

The years in Bermuda had enabled me to entrench myself in the "rut of comfort," but as years slipped away and the decades notched upwards, I felt strongly that adventure still called. What happened to the intrepid young woman saving up to buy a boat and sail to Greece? The horrid attack was the final shove that motivated me to make a life change—to change course completely. I felt I wanted to challenge myself, mentally, physically, and psychologically, and if I had a man along, well, the challenge would be there, but it would be completely different, as I would soon discover in Montreal.

Paul arrived to see if I had settled in and promised to take me to breakfast the next morning. Patrick stopped by to make sure I had been welcomed to the club marina as he had kindly made the booking for me. Mark and Marielle popped their heads in to say hello. They lived on a lovely steel schooner anchored nearby and offered me a ride to a supermarket the next day. Pierre came over from his nearby sports boat to say "bonsoir." Nicole issued a pressing invitation aboard their craft for cocktails. Lonely? No. Much too busy, actually.

*       *       *

A violent wake tossed *Dart* sideways and nearly flung me out of bed early the next morning. Hull and the Ottawa River were busy already. The marina adjoined the extensive grounds of the Canadian Museum of Civilization; the striking curved buildings with their unusual undulating design provided a splendid aspect across the river to Parliament Hill and the magnificent government buildings. I visited the museum and gazed in awe at the stunning collection of native totem poles and enjoyed the re-creation of Canadian history from the arrival of Vikings in 1000 AD to the advent of the French in the seventeenth century. But my main purpose was more prosaic. I discovered an excellent diner within the museum complex, and Tucker and I made a regular morning trek for a breakfast picnic of bacon and egg sandwiches, juice, and muffins. These we shared at a picnic table while appreciating the tranquil park and view.

We walked around the local town of Hull and found it to be an eclectic mixture of old factories, modest wood homes, and modern civic buildings. I discovered that the wood-framed houses were called "matchboxes" for a couple of reasons: They originally housed employees of the Eddy match factory and also had a tendency to burn down. So many buildings burned that few of historical note remain. Eddy matches may have lit the whole world, but they nearly burned down their entire homeland.

# CHAPTER TWELVE

# Sunset Encounter

The Carillon Lock had been the highlight of the day, providing a 65-foot drop from the Ottawa River to the Lac des Deux Montagnes. It was a busy weekend, and boats appeared from all directions to enter the lock. Four of the smallest craft, *Dart* included, rafted up across the front of the lock, and the bigger boats filled in behind us. The floating dock within the lock meant no one had the responsibility and worry of handling lock lines.

*The small boats,* Dart *included, rafted up at the front of the lock.*

It was a merry throng, and we chatted back and forth in English and French while tending our own and each others' lines as the boats jostled in position while the water drained from the lock and the level descended swiftly. I was still in long pants and sweat shirt, but the sturdy French sported bikinis and skimpy shorts. To them, summer was not a temperature but an attitude, and they were determined to enjoy it no matter how chilly.

*The vast gate at the head of the lock lifted up and revealed the lake.*

The vast gate at the head of the lock lifted up and revealed the broad expanse of the lake shining in the afternoon sun. We four small boats gradually untied from each other and peeled off and out of the lock, avoiding the drips from the overhead barrier. The bigger boats behind us charged past at full throttle, tossing us in their insane wakes. I motored along slowly, taking a careful look at the villages of Carillon and Pointe Fortune. The town docks fronted right onto the lake, and I knew the wakes from the speedboats would be unpleasant and maybe even dangerous, tossing small *Dart* against unrelenting concrete. That's when I decided to steam further onto the lake and try my luck at St. Placide. I ended up instead in the tranquility of a delightful, private yacht club.

The day had begun as I departed from the impressive Chateau Montebello, the largest log cabin in the world, now a Fairmont property. Staying there for a few days had really been a treat to myself. The marina was expensive, but I had the run of the hotel property and its many facilities. I took advantage of the swimming pool, the walking trails with Tucker, and a super barbecue dinner served on the hotel terrace. Guests arrived hourly in luxurious cabin cruisers and even by seaplane for dinner. I had been assigned to the small boat section of the marina and did not feel out of place while just across the way, mega-yachts posed proudly with uniformed deck hands.

A large French family arrived nearby in two Bayliner sport cruisers, and I could hear some sort of heated altercation. I gathered that they had requested adjoining berths and had been given two that were not together. Sizing up the situation, I walked over and offered to move my boat across to the next pier so they could be alongside each other. The French may argue vociferously, but they express their gratitude with equal enthusiasm. The entire group of 10, children included, were so appreciative they all joined in to take lines and pushed and pulled *Dart* over to one side with many a "merci, merci beaucoup, Madame!" When it was time for me to depart, the whole family—youngsters too—once again gathered in a group to untie my lines, push me away from the dock, and wave a cheerful and fond farewell as I set off.

I peered through the binoculars at St. Placide, the small French-Canadian village about half a mile away. Having decided against the two villages near the Carrillon Lock, *Dart* was now stationary in the still, calm water of the Laq des Deux Montagnes. We were hanging in nine feet of clear water, and I could see the sand and weed below. It had been a long and challenging day, and the petite village of St. Placide sounded like a great spot to spend the night. But where were the markers leading across the shallows into the town dock? The chart showed a row of buoys, but I couldn't see any of them on the lake. I spotted a small sailboat ahead of me, sails hanging lifeless, drifting in the idle air. It looked about *Dart*'s size, so I decided to head in the same direction.

The low coastline to the north of the village rose to a steep, sheer cliff that curved around the Baie de Saint-Placide to Pointe Aux Anglais. As I watched, the sailboat turned sharply in toward land and vanished. Intrigued, I took up the binoculars for a closer look. Just above the cliff peak and mingling with the tree tops were tips of masts, dozens of them, perhaps a hundred. Could there be a marina within the cliff? Tantalized, I pushed the throttle ahead, and we slid easily across the smooth, translucent surface of the lake. Cautiously, as the water shallowed, I steered around the front of the cliff between shore and a large, pseudo, black and white lighthouse. Yes, there was a narrow entrance, and within it I saw two lines of moored sailboats and a narrow channel between them leading to an attractive clubhouse with lawns and mature trees. There were only a few feet of water at the entrance but certainly enough for *Dart* and the array of small boats within.

As I steamed carefully down the slender channel, I noted boat owners chatting in French and English, some readying their craft for an outing, and others just returned and tidying up.

I turned neatly at the dock, tied up alongside, and walked up to the clubhouse. A handsome, white-painted clapboard building surrounded by a broad, shadowed porch lay at the back of a long, verdant lawn scattered with Adirondack chairs, picnic benches, and barbecues under deep, shady trees. Asking for the commodore, I met Jacques who was most hospitable and informed me that he had crewed in a Bermuda race many years previously. He pointed out a vacant berth that I might use since the owner was out sailing for a few days. Although the Club de Voile des Laurentides was a private club, they offered hospitality to visitors, and I was most glad to take advantage.

*The tranquility of the Club de Voile des Laurentides*

Jacques walked along the finger pier to meet and help me as I brought *Dart* over, and we secured her in a tiny gap. It was good to be off the lake and away from the endless wakes that flung *Dart* turbulently. I jumped overboard to cool off and tugged Tucker into the water with me. A delicious curry supper was washed down with some equally delightful chardonnay, and as twilight settled, Tucker and I walked out of the clubhouse grounds and into the surrounding residential neighborhood.

The sunset was magnificent. Had I painted it, I would have pulled out tubes of cadmium yellow and red, rose dore, alizarin crimson, lemon yellow, and magenta. The stunning gold and saffron dwindled into ruby, amethyst, and emerald. As Tucker lead the way along the dusky, country road, the huge oaks and chestnuts were silhouetted darkly against the glowing crimson and vermilion sky. From a low bungalow with a garden of evening, floral scents stepped an intriguing citizen, a petite woman of mature years wrapped in a silk robe, her silver hair, wet from a swim, combed neatly back.

"Bon soir, Madame," we exchanged. "Une belle soir, n'est ce pas?"

I told her I was from the club where I stayed on "mon petit bateau." She pointed to her "famille" on the property just across the narrow road from her house. The land sloped down to the lake, the mirrored water now shades of peach and coral reflecting the evening sky between the tall trees. In the center, a tepee bonfire of stacked wood crackled merrily, the flames picking up the sunset colors. A handful of traditional wood armchairs were gathered around, and I heard the chatter of low voices.

"Au 'voir, Madame. Bon nuit," I said.

She raised her hand graciously and bid me farewell. Tucker and I turned for home—*Dart*—and her snug cabin.

*          *          *

I stayed a second night at the Pointe aux Anglais in the neat little yacht club. I really hoped for another spectacular sunset and planned to have my camera ready this time. The day passed quietly as I polished brass and chrome industriously, cleaned the boat, napped, and read. Tucker, secure on her long line, sniffed happily along the waters edge and in the thick undergrowth on the steep banks, undoubtedly giving heart attacks to nearby nesting groundhogs. We walked the winding coast road and found the marina that I believed I had stumbled on when in fact, by good fortune, I discovered the yacht club.

There was no sunset to speak of, although I watched in anticipation, Olympus OM 2000 in hand. So instead, Tucker and I walked back along the coastal drive and enjoyed dinner on the marina terrace. Tucker was permitted to accompany me, and she sat quietly beneath the table and enjoyed nibbles and tastes of steak and cheesecake.

Next day dawned grey and cloudy with a blustery wind, not my favorite weather for an auspicious departure. *Dart* powered easily through the short, steep, peevish waves, and I calmed myself with assurance that I could, of course, turn and go back if wind and waves increased. They didn't, so I didn't.

I was sorry not to have the opportunity to visit Oka as I passed close by. The name Oka means "golden fish," and, I learned, it had a fascinating history, settled originally by Sulpicians who established a mission to convert local Indians to Catholicism. A village of French colonists developed nearby. Although now considered a suburb of Montreal, Indians still have a presence. In 1990 Mohawk warriors, women, and children barricaded the main road to protest a plan to develop part of their pine forest territory, including ancestral burial grounds, into a golf course. The "Oka Crisis" lasted 11 weeks and culminated with the Prime Minister sending thousands of troops to negotiate with a small band of Mohawks. The Indians surrendered reluctantly, but by then the event had created international interest, and in 1997 the federal government purchased the town of Oka and gave it back to the Mohawk community.

We locked through into St.-Anne-de-Bellevue, and Tucker and I strolled the narrow main street lined with quaint shops, boutiques, a pharmacy, and a hardware store. I discovered a small supermarket and stocked up with provisions. We returned to *Dart* just as a rain shower became a deluge, and I was glad to close the boat up snugly and fire up the stove. Bacon and chopped onion fried aromatically, and I tossed in the leftover curry for a tasty dinner. Tucker and I turned in early with a good book for me and a rawhide chew for her.

# CHAPTER THIRTEEN

## Lost on the Lake

I lost my way on Lac St. Louis.

It was only a two-minute motor from the town waterfront of St.-Anne-de-Bellevue to the nearest gas dock. It was midmorning, as I had delayed departure in order to attend the local farmers' market to stock up on home-made herb and olive bread, delicious chutney, and some local strawberry jam.

I docked carefully and waited a few minutes. As I stood by while the tank was filled, I glanced around and noted a motor cruiser emerging from what appeared to be a clump of trees on a bank just across the waterway. I casually inquired of the dock attendant, "Is that the entrance to the canal?"

"That's it," he confirmed.

Well, I thought to myself, it's just as well I stopped here. I had no idea the waterway turned into a bank of trees. Where would I have ended up? Probably embarrassingly aground 100 yards from the gas dock. I untied *Dart* and headed across to the willow-draped shoal and then spotted the correct channel markers on the narrow passage that would lead me into Lac St. Louis.

The lake revealed itself as broad, windless, and (thankfully) smooth but scattered with a profusion and confusion of markers, buoys, lights, flashers, and towers, many receding into the haze. There seemed to be at least five buoyed channels within the lake, and they all converged somewhere in the center. I knew where I was going, since I had carefully studied the chart and guide book. Heading confidently toward the Lachine Canal and then Montreal, I motored happily along on this warm, sunlit day, the bimini shading me and our own progress creating a cooling breeze. A sporty Bayliner drew alongside, briefly tossing me in its wake.

"Lachine?" the skipper called to me and pointed forward into my proposed route.

"Oui, oui," I responded in my best French.

He roared off at 50 knots bearing his cargo of bronzed, bikini babes. Five minutes later he was back, racing toward me and pulling up in a dramatic stop. He waved madly. "C'est Dorval, pas Lachine!" he called out.

Oh, shoot! I cursed myself and my overconfidence.

"Merci," I called and waved as the Bayliner shot off in another direction. Checking the chart book, I realized that the line of buoys I was following was fractured by a turn of a chart book page at a critical point. I had been heading quite the wrong way.

I turned *Dart* 'round, and we began retracing our steps along the line of markers. Thank heaven, it was a fine, calm day. Having to backtrack at five knots could throw the time frame completely off schedule. Back at a critical marker, I took a careful look around with binoculars and headed off on the course I should have taken. A large motor cruiser was coming toward me and slowed politely so I wasn't swamped with a huge wake. I took the opportunity to call them on the VHF and ask if I was on track for Lachine. They told me to look out for the tower marker mid-lake to make the next course change. I motored on and soon spotted the tower. I was amused to note at least half a dozen varied craft circling and calling out to each other. I could imagine the inquiries. "Which way to Dorval? Is this the route to Lachine? Where's St.-Anne-de-Bellevue?"

Feeling a little more confident, I carried on toward the entrance to the Lachine Canal. This canal had only recently been opened after major reconstruction. It led from the lake directly into Montreal and would save me many miles. It also bypassed a run on the St. Lawrence River with a contrary tidal flow of up to four knots. I didn't think that *Dart* would be able to risk that, so the Lachine was a benefit for me.

I docked on the blue line outside the first lock, joining a group of small craft—sport cruisers, mainly, with small family groups on board for the weekend. An official came out to measure us with a tee bar to ensure that our air draft was less than eight feet so we could pass under the low bridges. Our collection of about five small craft was called into the lock together, but as I steamed through the gates, the youthful lock master, perched on the top of the lock, called down to me, "How many aboard your boat?" he asked. Actually, he called out in French, and I was slow to translate and respond so he repeated in English.

"Just one," I replied.

"Sorry," he said, "You cannot pass through the canal with only one on board. You need two at least. You must turn around and leave."

Blow that, I thought to myself and called up to him.

"Sorry, I can't turn around right here." I was right in between the lock gates.

"Well, you must back out then," he shouted.

"Sorry," I called back. "This boat doesn't back too well."

"Don't worry," I added to reassure him, "I'll find someone to come with me."

Surely, I thought, I could borrow a friendly soul from another boat. I tied up against the floating dock within the lock under the disapproving stares of the lock staff. A quick glance revealed that each boat in the lock with me had only two adults on board. Oh, heck, now I'm in trouble, I thought. The lock staff stood back and refused to close the gates until all was legal and proper. Now I was holding up an entire lock full of boats.

I called up to the onlookers on the lock-side.

"Anyone come to Montreal with me?"

They gazed impassively down into the lock, shorts-clad sightseers draped with cameras; grannies in long, black dresses with parasols held high; kids with caps on backwards and trendy sneakers. An elderly man astride an old fashioned pedal bike with a French loaf protruding from the large wicker basket strapped to the handlebars leaned over.

"Well," he said, rather enigmatically, "I would go with you for sure, but my wife's in hospital."

The crews from the other waiting boats joined in the search and called around in French. One came dashing over to me.

"I've found you a crew," he said, excitedly.

*Lucy and Denise joined me for the trip through the Lachine Canal to Montreal.*

Thank heaven, here came Lucy and Denise clambering down the steep ladder into the lock, barefoot and carrying huge roller blades and armfuls of knee, elbow, and shin pads.

"We'd bladed far enough and stopped for a rest," they told me, "And, yes, we'd love to come on your boat to Montreal."

The lockkeeper began the locking process, and I settled Lucy and Denise on board. We practiced fractured French and English on each other, gradually gaining confidence in the other language. We had five locks to negotiate, so in each case, Lucy jumped ashore with the bow line, I followed with the stern line, and Denise switched the engine off and on again as required and kept an eye on Tucker. We had a three-hour traverse of the canal which lead us deeper into the city environs. We passed waterside parks, handsome townhouses, and old brick warehouses, many converted to waterside condos but others looking derelict and awaiting renovation. Speed was restricted to six knots which suited *Dart* just fine—no wakes to contend with and no anxious power boats trying to pass us. We shared the canal with dozens of tiny, blue, rental pedal boats, their occupants waving cheerfully as we passed. The waterside track was thronged with walkers, cyclists, and rollerbladers; couples with baby buggies or jogging strollers; and a multitude of leashed dogs. We ducked under very low bridges, and the five locks raised us gradually to the level of the St. Lawrence River and city of Montreal.

Lucy, slim and energetic, proved to be fiercely independent. She was an executive with a major corporation and had a career with huge responsibilities. Denise was warm and motherly and raising her nine year-old son alone but keeping an eye out for potential dates. The eventful day was coming to an end, and we tied up with much relief at the Port L'Escale right in downtown Old Montreal. To our right and left, long piers once used for ocean-going shipping now rang out with lively music while swarms of passers-by enjoyed boutiques and snack bars, slurping dripping ice cream cones and munching on mustard-drenched hot dogs.

Whole families rented tricycle pedal wagons or rode the sightseeing trolleys that swerved adroitly through the milling throng. It was a colorful scene and a dazzling contrast to the space and tranquility of the Lac St. Louis. The music of two live bands resonated between the long wharves. Eager crowds streamed up and down the long ramps to the water side parks to watch movies, shows, and fireworks. Boat owners from the extensive marina joined in with passengers who were flowing on and off the ferry boats, cruise ships, and sightseeing craft. Once a center of maritime activity, the harbor now teemed with visitors, not only tourists but also Montrealers enjoying the atmosphere of history and tradition and the choice of wonderful French restaurants, most with tables of enthusiastic diners spilling out onto the sidewalks and roadside terraces. Street performers entertained every few yards, and the waterfront park hosted numerous international exhibitions.

*We tied up with much relief at the Port L'Escale, right in downtown Montreal.*

Lucy and Denise refused payment for their afternoon as crew but accepted taxi fare home. They returned that evening, and we enjoyed dinner ashore at a trendy inn set in the charming, narrow, cobbled streets that form the Old Port. As I listened to the backdrop of excited French chatter, jazz bands, the clatter of dishes, and the clink of wine glasses, it was hard to believe that only that morning, I was lost on the lake.

Every day was an adventure. Each dawn brought new vistas, new villages, new friends, new acquaintances, and new experiences. I felt like a Christmas stocking, brimming with wonderful gifts.

# CHAPTER FOURTEEN

# The Co-pilot on Lake Champlain

"It's too shallow here! There's not enough water! You're going to run aground! I can see bottom!"

Barrie hopped nervously from one leg to the other from his perch on the bow. I ignored him and watched the depth sounder—eight feet, nine feet, plenty of water; good grief, I thought, what an irritating co-pilot I had on board with me! Barrie had flown from England to join me on the venturesome trek from Montreal through Lake Champlain. My apprehensive feelings about lakes were unchanged; Champlain was a big one, and I thought I would be glad for the company. On the other hand, I now had apprehensive feelings about Barrie. I needed to create physical and mental space within tiny *Dart* and within my psyche to accommodate a personality that threatened to overwhelm mine. Compromise was the watchword for the next couple of weeks as we struggled toward a balance of disposition and personality.

I admitted to myself that not too many weeks earlier, standing tearfully at the pay phone in Rome, I had begged him to come and join me, that I was scared and alone and couldn't cope. During the ensuing weeks, I became confident and competent and suddenly viewed with alarm the prospect of shared space and rival command. As we motored into one of the first locks, I had a helper on board, although by this time I was locking almost flawlessly. To my dismay, Barrie stood up wielding the boat hook, and as we motored between the lock gates, he pushed us away from the wall.

"Don't do that," I called. Actually, I think I shouted. This approach to Barrie was a bad choice. Alas, my crew flung the boat hook down and slumped into a sulk on the bow.

Tying up the boat suddenly became a challenge. On my own I would scan the approaching dock with binoculars and pick out the cleat or bollard to tie to. By now, I could pretty much place *Dart* right alongside the chosen point and stop the boat. Then it was easy to step ashore with the central spring line and toss the bow and stern lines onto the dock to be secured. Now I had a deck hand poised anxiously on the bow ready to leap ashore before the boat had stopped and hastily cleat off the bow line, leaving the stern to swing out into the stream. I clamped my jaws shut on many occasions. Barrie didn't take kindly to instruction or suggestion.

We pulled *Dart* alongside St. Denis' public dock in search of a cappuccino for Barrie, a daily necessity for him and found a traditional French-Canadian festival underway. The village center was thronged with stalls, stands, and booths selling an array of handmade crafts and foods. Jams and preserves, chutney and spices, aromatic herbal products, pottery and ceramics, lace and woolens, hand carved wood and scenic paintings were exhibited. The stall-holders were dressed in simple country costume, perfectly recreating an 18th century fiesta. We wandered from stall to stall, examining and commenting and dredging deep into our memory for enough schoolroom French verbs and nouns to muddle through conversation and questions. We didn't find the desired cappuccino but instead tucked into unusual French-style buckwheat pancakes and tasty lamb sausages.

When we set off again, we were loaded with extra sausages for dinner; fresh, un-shucked, locally-grown corn cobs; and scented candles. The Richelieu River was hectic with vacationing boaters, three-tiered mega-yachts, trendy speedboats, anchored craft strung with fishing rods, canoes, and row boats, all either producing vast wakes or combating them. This did not make for a relaxing day.

*We happened upon a Montgolfier at St.-Jean-de-Richelieu—100 balloons.*

Following our visit to St. Denis, we carried on to Saint-Jean-de-Richelieu where we happened upon a Montgolfier at the local air base. It was an amazing sight: 100 giant balloons being inflated and lofting into the evening sky simultaneously. All colors, designs, and shapes, they expanded and floated into a sunset sky. The air was filled with the roar of hot air machines and gasps of delight from the crowd as each new multi-hued balloon rose up from the grass and took wing as if to catch up with its soaring mates.

We were up the next day at 5:00 a.m. and set off by 6:00 a.m. on a tranquil, misty morning. As we turned to bid farewell to the town, we noticed all the balloons aloft again behind us, drifting above the river, setting off early for the scheduled day flight. We arrived at the U.S. border at noon and were cleared through at Gaines Marina in Plattsburg by a very personable and helpful customs officer.

We anchored off Valcour Island in Lake Champlain, but by afternoon the wind had kicked up such uncomfortable swells that we motored around the island to re-anchor in a sheltered cove enclosing a throng of other moored craft. It was a lovely bay, ringed with pines and cedars and a rocky shoreline with one long, shallow beach. Tucker enjoyed an energetic run on the island with Barrie.

I turned 61. I was not sure if this was a milestone to be mourned or celebrated. At age 60, one can commemorate the closure of a significant decade, but 61 seems such a trivial number. My 60th birthday was marked in grand style with family and close friends at a Bermuda garden party. But what a year it had been! I may not have felt like observing my birthday, but the year's adventures were more than enough to rejoice. Barrie and I marked the occasion in the handsome town of Burlington by eating and drinking too much—smoked salmon, brie, avocado, Pouilly Fuisse, a bottle of Gold Leaf dessert wine, and a selection of divine chocolate pastries. Quelle indigestion!

Our next stop was Essex—historic, charming, and full of character. We pulled into the local shipyard and were directed into a spare bay in the tiny, busy marina. Tucker was glad to be ashore again, and we wandered through the eccentric gift shops, tucked into ice cream, and reserved for dinner in the lakefront restaurant.

As we left Essex Shipyard, we had the usual disagreements.

"I'm going to turn *Dart* 'round," I announced.

"You don't have to do that," Barrie countered. "Just back her out under power; you'll be fine."

I looked around at the jam-packed marina and knew only too well what a calamity that could be. I'd tried maneuvering her under power before with disastrous results. Standing on the dock, I eased *Dart* gently out to the end of the little wooden pier, then tugged her stern around using the dock corner and a fender as pivot. Once she was safely facing straight out of the busy marina, I stepped on board and powered out. Barrie remained below, irritated.

*The Champlain Bridge was silhouetted against the Green Mountains.*

The Champlain Bridge was silhouetted against a flippant bank of cloud that hovered hesitantly over the Green Mountains. Barrie was packed and ready to catch the afternoon train to New York for his flight to England. Why was it that when it was almost time for him to depart, he became amenable and agreeable, and suddenly we were a congenial pair? Then I felt guilty that I wanted him gone. I wondered, perhaps I should ask him to stay on? There was still a long trek ahead south down the lake and through the Champlain River and Canal.

Finally, with just minutes to spare, I ventured hesitantly, "So... do you want to stay another week?"

"I was just thinking the same thing," he replied. "Sure. Why not?"

He cheerfully flung his bag back into the boat. I started the engine, and we headed south.

The Champlain River was wonderfully curvaceous, flowing calmly south between the majestic Adirondacks on our right and the lofty Green Mountains of Vermont facing them. At Chipmans Point, we found two stately, historic warehouses converted to marina use. The interior of the facility building was the original rough stone wall, whitewashed and decorated with border trims, dried flowers, and antiques. Dick and his wife, both energetic and white-haired, had created a homely domain for themselves and their visitors.

"I guess it's really quiet in the winter," I ventured to Dick.

"No, indeed, it's even busier," he said to my surprise.

At my startled reaction, he explained that once the floating docks and moorings have been pulled out of the river in the fall, all the boats have been lifted onto land, and the lake has frozen, it becomes a thoroughfare.

"We have snowmobiles, cars, and even trucks using it as a highway," he said.

*As the day progressed, the rain increased. Barrie insisted we leave.*

By morning, the wind had increased and swung to the north, directly behind us. At 5:00 a.m. the entire marina was rattling, floating docks bouncing, rigging slapping, and shroud and stay wires humming. *Dart*'s rudder and tiller crashed noisily back and forth, and I decided to turn her around to face the weather. Barrie argued worriedly against it.

"Why try and move the boat? It's too risky and difficult, and we're leaving soon anyway," he complained.

"Well," I retorted, "it's my boat, and I want to turn her 'round. I'll do it myself."

I ran a line from her bow cleat, around the bow, and secured it to a cleat on the dock. I set another long line from the outside stern cleat, also right around the bow, and laid it on the dock ready to tighten up. I cast off the stern line and hung onto the bow platform, and the wind carried the stern right around. The new lines were already in place to hold her securely in her new position. *Dart* and I rested more comfortably until we were ready to cast off and head down the Champlain River.

The next day we awoke to a gloomy, overcast sky and sputtering rain and set off at 8:00 a.m. As the day progressed, the rain increased until by Lock 1 it was teeming down, and we were both soaked and shivering. We had five big drop locks through the dank, damp, tree-draped canal. I was genuinely glad to have help with these difficult locks with a stern wind pushing us awkwardly. On the other hand, it was Barrie who insisted we leave. Up at 5:00 a.m. as usual, he'd been itching to cast off. Left to myself, I'd have stayed under my cozy quilt with a good book and waited all day if necessary for better weather.

We arrived at Waterford at 4:30 p.m. and jumped into hot showers, laundered masses of wet clothing, and then set off to Kielty's Irish Pub for huge plates of pork chops and local fresh vegetables, good red wine, and a sense of repletion and achievement. I had just crossed my outward track, May 24-August 30, 2002, a memorable occasion.

There was an excellent rail service to New York from Albany, and Barrie was ready to disembark there. This time I did not suggest he stay on. We had lurched from dilemma to crisis and back several times but survived the voyage and remained friends. There was no emotional farewell for me. I was glad to be in control again. I could get up in the morning when I chose instead of 5:00 a.m., eat late if I liked, read, walk Tucker—all on my own time. It was good to be back in charge of my life.

Barrie set off for the train station. The tide was pinning me firmly against the dock at Albany Yacht Club, so I put the kettle on, made a cup of tea, waited until the tide turned and the sun burned off a duvet-thick fog bank, and set off, happily single again, south, down the Hudson River.

# CHAPTER FIFTEEN

## My Second Year Afloat—Blunders

"WOOOoooooooooo"

The blast of a horn echoed across the river and seemed to emanate from beyond the encircling Hudson Highlands, indeed from heaven itself. Was Poseidon sounding the alarm?

Dragged violently from my reverie, I looked ahead in some dismay and quickly pushed the tiller over, turning *Dart* sharply to starboard. Ahead and bearing down fast was a vast tow with a tug pushing from behind, charging right toward me. Good grief, I thought. What other stupid mistake am I to make today?

Just minutes before I had noted what appeared to be a tall light structure on a small island. Glancing quickly at the chart, I confirmed that I could probably pass either side of the light. I was musing as I considered which side of the "light" to pass, port or starboard. As we neared, I noted white wavelets lapping at the foot of the "rocks." Must be quite a tide running, I thought. Wrong! What I had identified as a light structure was the tall steering bridge deck of the tug tucked in behind the huge barge he was pushing, bow wave frothing fiercely.

The skipper's warning blast alerted me in good time to take avoiding action and provide him with all the clearance he needed. I kept my head down as we passed and imagined him thinking, silly old dear, she really shouldn't be on the river.

Only minutes later came blunder number three.

This time I was paying better attention, and while Wraith, my auto helm, steered, I kept a careful watch with the binoculars. I could see beneath the Kingston-Rhinecliff Bridge, and that's when I spotted the freighter in good time. But why was she hugging the coast as she entered Barrytown Reach?

I checked the chart and gulped. The Flat! Oh, shoot! I was right over it. I glanced at the depth gauge, only five feet of water! The tiller was pushed hard over as we headed quickly to port and back into 36 feet of deep river. Little Miss Ego decided to have a serious talk with me.

"If you can't do better than this, you'd better turn around right now, go home, and get a job in a shop," she chided. "You've one season of cruising under your garters, and I expect better of you. You're a seasoned boater now. Prove yourself."

Perhaps a winter in Bermuda had caused a lapse in attention and judgment. It was fun being home surrounded by family and friends and enjoying a cheerful Christmas season in my own waterside condo. But at the back of my mind, I visualized *Dart*, abandoned, moored alone in a dismal New Jersey marina, grey with city grime and drenched with wintry rain. Marina neighbors sent me photographs of my brave little craft almost invisible under a cloak of hoary snow. The months passed swiftly, and by the following May, Tucker and I flew back into New York, returned to our pocket-sized floating abode, and set off for further adventures.

It was then that I had my first lapse in attention. Day one of my second voyage, and I found myself involved in a tug of war with a rope snarled around the propeller.

It was Saturday, a grey, gloomy, overcast morning with rain clouds gathering threateningly and the occasional sputter of rain and spray. I was determined to head out of my New Jersey marina and onto the river today to avoid the turmoil of fast commuter ferries that terrorize small boaters on weekdays. I pulled on my yellow rain pants and zipped up my waterproof jacket. It felt a bit unwieldy, but I wanted to keep warm and dry. The river was dreary and bland, but my spirits were alive with elated anticipation.

This was the start of year two of my adventure, and with increased confidence and assurance, I was setting off once more, having left behind me a conflagration of charred bridges this year. My tour business had been sold, my apartment rented, personal possessions in storage. This year was serious. I was on my own with no way back.

I crossed the river from the Jersey shore to gain a lee from the brisk west wind and was amused to spot the plump rumps of three Bermuda-bound cruise ships moored on the Manhattan side, familiar shapes awaiting an influx of fresh passengers. As I glanced backwards for a farewell glimpse of the Manhattan skyline, I blanched. The green oil pressure light on the outboard engine was not shining reassuringly at me. It had gone out. Good grief! My first day out alone, and something was disconcertingly and definitely not right.

Leaving Wraith in charge, I ducked below, pulled the settee cushions frantically aside, dug into a locker, and pulled out the Yamaha engine operating manual.

*I spotted the plump rumps of three Bermuda-bound cruise ships,
moored on the Manhattan side.*

"If green light goes out, stop engine immediately, check oil level or call your local Yamaha dealer."

It seemed that option B was out, so I elected option A. But where to stop? One of the empty cruise ship bays at Pier 40 seemed to offer public access. With the binoculars, I swept the docks. One side was too high and one side too low to dock easily, but there were a number of floating buoys, all empty. I decided to pick up a buoy, tie off, and check the oil.

Thanks to the tide rushing up the river, I missed the first two buoys I tried to capture with the boat hook. I was luckier with the third as it swept by me. I snared it and tied a stern line to the ring on top of the buoy. Somewhat hampered by the full set of foul weather gear, I leaned out across the outboard engine and managed to release the cover. Lifting it off, I recalled the position of the oil tank and pulled out the dipstick. I wiped it off with a paper towel and thrust it back in. Whew! There was plenty of oil. Relieved, I replaced the engine hood, started the engine, pulled my line aboard, and pushed the gear control into forward. With an ugly jerk and thud, *Dart* came to a sudden stop, and the engine went horribly silent. What now? The buoy was still alongside, so I quickly threaded a line through the ring once more and peered over the side.

A stout line attached to the buoy and hanging covertly down in the grubby water had been efficiently picked up by my propeller. I pulled at the attached end, but it was firmly entwined.

*I sawed off the offending line with the bread knife and flung it into the cockpit.*

Here's one occasion where an outboard scores, I thought; thank heaven I don't have to dive overboard. I got out the lever that tilts the heavy engine and heaved it up. Without the lever, it's impossible to lift the 90-pound weight. A black, slimy, one-inch-thick line was firmly wound around the prop shaft. I managed to unwind a foot or so, but the last few inches were squeezed tightly between the prop and shaft. By now I was steaming with anxiety and frustration, and sweating within the rain suit. I couldn't reach the prop to cut the line off. But I had one last idea. I switched on the engine and gave it a one-second burst of power in reverse. It worked! The rope untwisted and sprang free. I was so mad at this point, I leaned over the side with the bread knife, sawed the hanging line off the buoy, and flung it into the cockpit.

I was pleased with myself for getting out of trouble, even if I got myself into it in the first place. If only I had checked the oil level before I set off.

# CHAPTER SIXTEEN

# Into the Trent-Severn...

On either side of us were the wetlands of the Trent-Severn Waterway, with rippling banks of slender, russet reeds, undulating rafts of mauve and ivory water lilies, and behind them deep groves of flowering trees wafting a wonderful perfume across the river. The poplars were seeding milk-white cotton balls that drifted with the breeze and settled and swayed on the surface in a light snowfall. They snared in adjacent trees, entangled in the grass and bushes, and reminded me of sheep's wool snagged in the hawthorn hedges, rustic fences, and stone walls of the English countryside. There was a smell of manure as we passed a farming community of barns and silos, throngs of contented cattle munching silage barely glancing up as we motored past. A pair of giant terns flew low overhead, focused on a distant destination.

I did well with Canadian locks that day. I was a bit nervous at first, but I knew I had to get used to picking up two cables.

In the U.S. locks, I could use one central line from the boat to secure *Dart* to the vertical cable or pipe. But in the Canadian locks they prefer you to pick up two cables, bow and stern. I soon became adept at this. I'd steam slowly past the first cable, snare a line 'round it, and quickly tie it back onto the stern of the boat; then I'd swiftly step forward onto the bow and with the boat hook grab the second cable and bend a line around that. Clinging to that line, I'd return to the first line, switch off the engine, and sit back to hang onto both lines while the lock filled. It was really sensible to have two lines; since the old-fashioned, English-style locks filled from one end, and the water rushed toward the boat so powerfully, it could force the bow well away from the lock wall and endanger other craft.

I once entered a lock full of boats already secured and had an audience for my performance. I did well and appreciated the admiring glances. Then the lockkeeper called down:

"I need the small sailboat to move forward, please."

My boating neighbors chuckled and called out to me, "You did so well, now let's see you do it again!"

I did, and they did.

\*　　　　　　　\*　　　　　　　\*

*Dart* and I were now heading west toward Georgian Bay, having turned out of the Bay of Quinte on Lake Ontario at Belleville, then ducked down the coast to Trenton, the start of the Trent-Severn.

We had successfully retraced our steps from Liberty Landing in New Jersey, up the Hudson River, along the Erie Canal, and up the Oswego Canal.

My second crossing of Lake Ontario went well as I had the company of my ex-husband George. He told me before I left home in May, "I don't like the idea of you crossing that lake on your own."

"Well," I replied, "in that case you'd better come with me."

*George, a retired boat captain, crossed Lake Ontario with me.*

He joined me for a few days, and I couldn't have asked for better company than a professional boat captain. During our years of marriage, we operated a small, wooden, glass-bottom boat, then a 60-foot stern paddle-wheeler. I handled the reservations and books, and George operated and maintained the boat. Perhaps the stress factors of being in business together formed the wedge that eventually split us apart. But we remained friends.

I awaited his arrival at Winter Harbour Marina in Brewerton, where Tucker fell madly in love with an Irish terrier called Sparky.

I collected George at Syracuse airport where he arrived with a marine shopping list for his own boat. We were fogged in for a few days in Oswego, so he accomplished most of his purchases thanks to Wal-Mart and an excellent local bus service. The weather cleared; the forecast promised a clear, smooth day; and during the 10-hour crossing of Lake Ontario, George read, napped, and cooked for most of the journey while I kept an eye on the chart and course, the engine, and fuel consumption.

I promised myself that while he was aboard with me, we would walk more and eat less. That worked for about two days; then I gave up the aspiration and agreed to eat more and walk less. We rode the marina bicycles and visited the local bars, pubs, and bakeries in Oswego, Kingston, and Belleville. By the time he caught the train to Toronto and his flight back to Bermuda, I think we had both quite happily gained a few pounds.

As soon as he left, the weather changed, and I had quite a night in Belleville. The movement of the boat woke me at 2:30 a.m., and I looked outside. The wind was picking up, and *Dart* was thrashing up and down and banging against the dock. I put a jacket on over my pajamas; dug out my lovely, new, pink 75-foot line; and leaning into the wind, walked it around to the dock opposite. I secured it to hold *Dart* away from our dock, felt happier then, and went right back to sleep.

I woke again at 5:30 a.m., and although it was a grey, gloomy day with a brisk breeze, I decided to head out. There was a two-foot chop on the surface, but *Dart* cut right through it with just a bit of spray on the boat. In two hours we turned off the Bay of Quinte and into Trenton. I tied up, and Tucker and I headed ashore for breakfast at the recommended waterside cafe. No one seemed to be serving, but the few locals tucking into aromatic breakfasts advised me to help myself to coffee and that Joe would be along soon. It was a long narrow cafe, fronting onto the casual main street and backing onto the waterway. Tucker settled down outside, secured to a tree.

When Joe turned up, he showed me pictures of his own Jack Russell and insisted on serving Tucker her ration of bacon on a paper plate.

We cast off and headed deep into the Trent-Severn Waterway, cruising slowly along beside cottages, mobile homes, motor homes, tents, shacks, and shanties, all inventively decorated. A large plastic white swan was filled with geraniums, miniature windmills whirled incessantly, gnomes, and odd shaped rocks had been painted and set across the lawns. We passed homes strewn with picnic tables and chairs, barbecues, jet skis, canoes, speedboats, pontoon boats, home-made docks and piers, pedal boats, and entire families of realistic ducks. Then we came to the upscale camps featuring elegant ranch style homes with spacious patios and terraces, enclosed swimming pools, greenhouses, tennis courts, miniature barns and playhouses, groups of classic Adirondack chairs, pergolas, ride-on lawn mowers, water slides into the lake, and jet skis in special launch pads.

We had a relaxing stop at lock six, a pleasant picnic area. I made sandwiches and sat under an oak tree while Tucker poked about at the end of her long, red line. We'd only seen two other boats that day, so it had been a

*I made sandwiches while Tucker poked about on the end of her red line.*

quiet morning. The lock master told me the first boat went through at 1:30, and we locked in at 2:30. I guessed July 1 would see the opening of the busy season, and I was running ahead of the crowd.

Turtles were sunning themselves on the bank as we passed through Danger Narrows, and the waterway made a 180 degree turn. I thought a turtle was swimming ahead of me so I slowed, but the small head protruding from the surface turned out to be a snake sinuously gliding across the river. We came to an area where the waterway split off to Richardson Cove, and we carried straight on with islands and rocks to our right and hills behind. A huge dead tree had floated downstream, lodged itself on the shoreline rocks, and was covered in turtles sunning themselves on a very comfortable resting place. The engine seemed to be running fine now, steaming along at half throttle, happily enough. I just had to listen carefully to it as I slowed down or took it out of gear as it tended to cut out, disconcerting when I was about to dock or tie up in a lock. I probably needed to adjust the idle screw. I surprised myself at my casual attitude. Last year I'd probably have panicked if the engine cut out. Now, it's just a nuisance.

Then, as I was half-listening to the engine, I heard sharp, cracking noises which really alarmed me; I wondered if there was a branch caught in the propeller or something ghastly happening in the carburetor. I soon realized, to my relief, it was just Tucker down below in the cabin, snacking heartily on a huge beef bone she had been given by dockside neighbors.

# CHAPTER SEVENTEEN

# The Squall and the Sunburn

I set off for Cambellford and enjoyed the camaraderie of the lockkeepers who kindly passed me along from one to the next. They each communicated with the next lock to advise how many boats to expect for the next locking and whether to ready the lock for rise or fall. Many times I was greeted with, "So, you're the lady from Bermuda, and this must be Tucker."

*I met Lily, the Jack Russell terrier belonging to the lockkeeper.*

At one lock, I met Lily, the Jack Russell terrier belonging to the lockkeeper. She bounced, bounded, and raced non-stop, leaping about the lock-side, springing onto the picnic table, and sprinting to the lockkeeper's house in an endless round of energy. She made Tucker seem like a staid old lady (like her owner, perhaps). I inquired about an outdoor concert coming up at a nearby park and wondered if I would be permitted to take Tucker along.

"If not, then you let me know, and we'll arrange a dog-sitter for you," the kindly lockkeeper promised.

A couple of locks further along the waterway, the lockkeeper inquired, "I hear you may need a sitter for Tucker. You just let me know, and we'll arrange something for you."

I dare say that only in Canada do lockkeepers provide dog-sitting service.

$$*\qquad\qquad*\qquad\qquad*$$

The Trent River surprised me—wide and windy with a brisk northeaster greeting me dead on the nose. *Dart* pounded readily into the unexpected waves, and I was soon drenched with spray. I quickly donned full foul weather gear as huge, ghastly, yellow and black storm clouds boiled up threateningly ahead. Lightning forked a dramatic warning across the dark hills; then thunder growled and grumbled. It started to sprinkle heavily, individual drops spattering on *Dart*'s decks and cabin top. Then came serious rain, torrential rain, and a howling white squall came whipping around the bend toward me at top speed, eclipsing the view ahead.

I was in a curving, narrow, marked channel with rocks close by on both sides. The markers disappeared into the deluge, and the rain, now horizontal, was so fierce it slashed my face and blinded me. I pushed the helm hard over to try to turn quickly in the narrow channel. *Dart* was flung hard over onto her side, and I clung onto the tiller, braced my feet against the seat, and was thankful that Tucker was safely below decks. As we gradually inched around, I glimpsed a small, snug cottage on the shoreline encircled by wind-whipped trees and wondered if they were anxiously watching my imminent demise. *Dart* gradually made the turn, righted herself, and with the wind-blown spume and rain now from behind, I could at least see where I was going. I idled the engine and let the fierce wind blow us back down the channel.

Now I could vaguely see the buoys. I thought of ducking behind a nearby island to anchor for shelter but decided to continue running back down through the markers. As quickly as it arrived, the rain eased away, the clouds cleared, and the squall passed on, rumbling its way up the river. I pushed the tiller over, and *Dart* reversed direction again. I then noticed that the island that might have provided shelter had only about two feet of water off the channel. The tips of reeds were growing up through the surface. It would not have been a propitious moment to run aground.

By 4:00 p.m. we arrived at the next lock, and I was glad to tie up, pull off wet clothes, light the upturned flowerpot on the propane stove to warm up, and make a cup of tea. I felt the sort of invigorating warmth that comes from a plunge into an ice-cold pool after an hour in the sauna. The squall had passed, leaving contentment and yet exhilaration. It was good to pull *Dart*'s comforting shawl about me once again.

By evening, the sky cleared, the sun came out, and I fixed a delicious meal of potato salad, smoked salmon, lots of mushrooms, and coleslaw, all in the same pot.

*         *         *

A long day lay ahead with the crossing of Rice Lake. I was suffering from "lake-anxiety" as usual as the lake was 20 miles long and two miles wide. There was a brisk wind, about 10-12 knots with one-foot waves. I was a trifle dry-mouthed, but *Dart* was doing beautifully, shouldering her way across the lake, the engine purring, Wraith, my auto helm, steering while I focused on the marked channel. I soon relaxed, quelled the apprehension, and enjoyed the voyage.

Three birds shared the sky above me. An osprey, giving his distinctive clear whistle, carried a huge silver fish in his talons. A belted kingfisher shook a spray of water drops off his blue crest as he surfaced, and a red-beaked tern competed with the others. All three dove companionably in the same area. They seemed to know where the shoals of minnows were. Fishermen in small boats, anchored on both sides of the channel, were probably angling for walleye and bass.

Rice Lake is famous for fishing and originally for the once-extensive wild rice beds, harvested by native tribes. The Southern Woodland people, descendants of the Paleo-Indians, camped near the wild rice beds 4,000 years ago. I decided to pay my respects by cooking up a pot of wild rice for dinner that night. I bought and studied Lorraine Brown's excellent book *The Trent-Severn Waterway—An Environmental Exploration*" and learned about alvars and eskers, drumlins and kames, gniesses and hypsithermal intervals. I was conscious that I had spent days—no, weeks—cruising in ignorance of the landscape around me and was now determined to rectify this deficiency.

I discovered the little egg-shaped islands we passed were drowned drumlins. (The word "drumlin" comes from a Celtic word meaning little hill, orientated northeast to southwest, illustrating the direction of the glacial passage that created them eons ago.) The Trent-Severn has a rich human history. Its value as a transportation route and source of plentiful wild life was recognized by Paleo-Indians who settled the area almost as soon as the glaciers disappeared from Southern Ontario 12,000 years ago.

Native peoples are still present along the Waterway, and we passed Chippewa and Mississauga communities on Rice, Scugog, and Buckhorn Lakes and on Lakes Simcoe and Couchiching. I passed Harris Island, two small drumlins with wild rice beds between the islands. Now a nature reserve, the island is forested with sugar maple, red oak, white ash, white pine, and aspen.

The lake was almost behind me, and I heaved a sigh of relief as I looked out for the flashing red marker for the turn into the Ontonabee River. There was a red post well ahead of me off to one side of the course, and I approached cautiously for identification. On closer inspection with the binoculars, the marker revealed itself to be a small, anchored motor boat containing a tall, scarlet man exhibiting a severe sunburn and not much else.

I gave him a wide berth.

# CHAPTER EIGHTEEN

# One Big Shoe Store

Another lake was thankfully behind me, and I could relax as I steered *Dart* through the meandering Ontonabee River. We twisted and turned for 20 miles before reaching Peterborough, where I decided to spend Canada Day and enjoy the stimulation of big city life for a couple of days.

We arrived at Peterborough Marina at 4:30 p.m., and I was directed to tie between the long public dock, thronged with sightseers, and a huge houseboat occupied by three vacationing couples who considered me a little too close for comfort. They hung up large, colorful beach towels with pegs in a vain attempt to create a little privacy. Dozens of voyeurs paced along the dockside and peered into *Dart*'s secluded cabin. This was not promising to be a peaceful location. I walked about the marina and found small boat dockage to the rear and was granted permission to move back. I was much happier to be where I had privacy and was moored with other small boats.

Tucker and I walked downtown, and she lay patiently at the entrance to the Stone House Restaurant on Main Street. I enjoyed fish and chips and an excellent local beer while Tucker enjoyed meeting everyone who entered or left the restaurant.

The marina adjoined the huge public park which hosted Canada Day celebrations with a vast array of ethnic food stands. Tucker and I wandered and grazed happily on Indian, Chinese, Turkish, Spanish, and local cuisine. A nap was followed by a walk and swim in the lake for Tucker. She was keen to scatter the sizeable flock of Canada geese wandering around the edge of the lake. I managed to deter her, but these flocks of domesticated wild geese are considered a nuisance by many small towns. They looked engaging and ecological, but the mess they left behind was repugnant. They deposited in their wake a broad swath of bright green guano that ruined beaches and spoiled grass picnic areas.

The Festival of Lights Celtic concert in the park was well attended by a happy family crowd sprawled across the extensive hillside facing down onto the outdoor staging. April Verch and her lively band put on a memorable performance. Park Rangers came by and told me Tucker was not permitted in the park, so I folded up my chair, and we returned to the boat. *Dart*'s cockpit provided an excellent view of the celebratory fireworks while I enjoyed coffee and a dozen delicious mini-donuts from the food stands.

I wondered how my children were, what they were up to this evening, did they miss me, or did they assume that Mum was okay. I knew they had every confidence in my ability, and I was beginning to feel the same.

*              *              *

Ahead lay the Peterborough Lift Lock, the highest hydraulic lift lock in the world and a new experience for me. When we reached the lock, I tied up alongside the dock at the waiting area and walked up to the visitor center and museum. This gave me a chance to watch boats using the lock and learn something about it. An amazing structure that looked modern but was 99

*Ahead lay the Peterborough Lift Lock, the highest hydraulic lift lock in the world.*

years old, it was going to lift me 65 feet. Two huge pans or boat pens alternated the ride up or down, counterbalancing each other. When it was time to lower the upper pan, extra water was pumped into it and the weight dropped it down.

Having watched for a while and calmed myself down sufficiently, it was my turn to motor into the strange contraption. It was easy and straightforward, and I tied *Dart* onto the side rails. As we rose, I had a splendid view but only a few minutes to admire it before the pen jolted to a halt, the front barrier slid down, and I was advised by loudspeaker to exit. I untied and pulled away into the Kawarthas, also known as cottage country.

We locked through Young's Point and Burleigh Falls and through Stoney Lake. Gradually, the scenery changed. By the time I eased into Buckhorn Yacht Harbor, I was wind- and sun-burned and ready to stop. We tied up to refuel and inquired about overnight. I was shocked a bit at the minimum charge but then pulled around the point beyond the marina and into a shallow lagoon behind it. I was a bit disconcerted to find that my fee did not include power or bathrooms, and Tucker was not allowed on the grass. However, a resident boat-owner kindly invited me to plug into his power outlet, and the marina manager told me that if I tiptoed discreetly into the "facility chalet," it would be "OK."

Tucker needed some exercise so we set off to find the "sandpit" which turned out to be a vast, disused quarry filled with a few feet of water. Tucker thoroughly enjoyed herself chasing minnows in the shallows while I sat in the water, cooled off, and chatted with a couple of mums with a brood of happy, splashing youngsters.

We disconnected early, steered cautiously out of the shallow pool, and enjoyed a nice morning's run to Bobcaygeon. The marina I had earmarked was not what I had hoped for. It was rather untidy and filled with small local runabouts. I carried on and was lucky enough to find a small, wooden dock near the town waterfront. We had our own lawn, picnic bench, and lovely spreading spruce trees alongside. When I tied Tucker ashore on her line, she rolled happily in the long grass and lay on her back in the shade of a giant Christmas tree.

Bobcaygeon was a bustling little community and a popular tourist resort, with upscale shops, boutiques, and a great supermarket. Ice cream and shoes featured high on the list of essentials along the pleasant, brick sidewalks decorated with hanging baskets of scarlet geraniums and purple petunias. I had been advised that Bobcaygeon was the place for shoes, and this proved to be true. Racks of bright canvas sneakers, bundles of colorful flip-flops, and baskets of beach shoes spilled out onto the sidewalks, and the windows beckoned with displays of elegant Italian court shoes, chunky Nikes, and sturdy Rockports. I found shoe stores on every street and street corner, and the intriguing thing was, if you went inside one, you could walk through to another and yet another—just one big shoe store.

*Tucker rolled happily in the long grass in the shade of a Christmas tree.*

The town, I learned, was listed as one of Canada's top ten places to retire, and I could understand this as I sat in *Dart*'s cockpit and watched the townspeople, many grey-haired or grey-bearded, licking vanilla and chocolate ice cream cones as they ambled along the congenial boulevards and reviewed the shoes for sale.

I found myself strolling the quiet streets and waterside walks, sharing an ice cream cone with Tucker, and realizing with dismay I was beginning to act like a retiree. But I wasn't ready to drop anchor for good, and retirement did not feature in my near future. Before I slowed down any further, I untied *Dart*, pushed away from our pleasant little dock, and headed west once more.

# CHAPTER NINETEEN

# Lake Simcoe to the Pacific

Lake Simcoe lay ahead, and I was already apprehensive. The shallow, fresh water lakes have a fearsome reputation for sudden storms producing short, steep seas that can overwhelm a small boat. The guide book warned me: "The major concern is to get across Lake Simcoe without getting beat up." Beat up? The delicate hairs on the back of my neck rose up in protest at the thought of the 16-mile crossing.

There was a sheltered pool with protective piers at the exit from the canal system where boats could await a propitious moment to cross the lake. The swing bridge opened to let *Dart* through, and I steered through the piers and out onto the lake. There was an uncomfortable chop on the water and a menacing, gusty breeze. The far shore was out of sight, and the horizon looked lumpy. I knew that a lumpy horizon meant there were big waves out there. I turned *Dart* 'round, returned to the pool, and tied up inside the pier to see if the wind would ease off during the afternoon.

The breakwater, built of huge boulders topped with a grassy walkway, seemed like a safe place to let Tucker run free. She wandered off happily, but only minutes later I heard a terrifying row, hysterical screams, angry barks, piercing yelps, and ferocious growls. I raced out onto the breakwater where several feet below me near the waterline, a hideous fight was taking place. The echoing, alternate screams and barks were Tucker, and the growls were from some wild creature in a secret lair. They were both buried out of sight in the caves and caverns formed by the boulders.

I shouted in vain. There was silence. Now I was really scared. Had Tucker been killed? I could never rescue her or find her torn and mangled body from deep within the rocks. There was a small sound behind me, and I turned. There stood a trembling and hesitant Tucker, a few specks of blood on her white whiskers. Relieved and thankful, I snapped on her lead, returned to the dock, cleaned her up, and secured her line to a nearby tree close by the boat.

A small sailboat, about *Dart*'s size, pulled in and moored against the wall on the far side of the pool. I kept a wary eye on the single occupant, thinking if he set off, I might follow him. Eventually, I called out, "Where are you headed, and when are you leaving?"

"I was waiting to see if you left. I'd follow you," came the shout.

"Not tonight, that's for sure," I called back.

The wind did not abate, and at dusk I motored back through the bridge and turned off the canal into a narrow creek I had noticed earlier. Huge pine, fir, and spruce trees leaned over the mysterious, shadowy waterway, and the overwhelming and nostalgic aroma was pure Christmas. Twisting and turning carefully down the slender, shallow inlet, we reached a tiny, local marina where I spent a tranquil night dreaming of Santa Claus, tinkling bells, and gold-wrapped gifts.

Morning brought an increase in wind, and back at the bridge, I could see without going further a convoy of white-capped waves marching resolutely across the lake. I backtracked up to the lock and asked to spend the day at the park above the lock.

"Well now, Ma'am," the lockkeeper said. "You paid your way down, but I'll have to charge you to go back up."

"That's OK," I said, "I'm happy to pay. I just want to wait until the wind on the lake dies down."

"In that case," he advised, "go back up to Thorah lock. It's much quieter there, and we won't charge you. Have a great day."

*Tucker and I spent a serene day at the lock-side park.*

Tucker and I spent a serene day at the lock-side park watching hordes of small family sport boats head down through the locks and bravely out onto the lake. Within the hour, they started to return.

"Man, it's rough out there," said one boater, both he and his wife pale with fright and drenched with spray. "There must be four foot waves, and there's no way I'm trying to beat that. I think you've got the right idea. We're staying here, too." They threw up their sun awning, set out the barbecue, and opened a couple of cold beers.

A herd of sedate, black and white cows munched reflectively in the field alongside us, content within the shade of the single giant chestnut. Blue Chicory and golden Meadow Buttercup nestled among the stately Queen Anne's Lace bordering the rustic track alongside the canal. Vast rolls of newly harvested hay balanced expectantly in the spacious fields below. Barn swallows dipped and swerved, chasing stray insects on the wing.

Tucker, secure in her harness and long line, was "spronking" happily in the long grass alongside the dock. I chuckled as I watched her but never could figure out how she knew where to make the sudden upward leap to land on all four paws, her nose right on top of some small prey. I listened obsessively to the marine forecast on the VHF radio and figured the weather the following day sounded feasible.

*Crossing Lake Simcoe with Doug and Elaine's Nordic Tug,* Bravo.

At 5:00 a.m., I dropped *Dart*'s short, red mast so I could steam under the low bridge, and together with neighbors Doug and Elaine on their Nordic Tug *Bravo*, we set off across the lake. Dawn tinted the demure horizon and unruffled vanilla water with shades of rose and lemon. A gaggle of small, swift gulls wheeled past me, their wings, as they banked in unison in the early sun, flashed like golden sparks. The breeze was fresh and invigorating, the motor was running smoothly, and *Dart* plowed happily through the diminutive wavelets. I felt confident and exuberant. I felt as though I could continue on forever.

I could cross the Pacific.

# CHAPTER TWENTY

# A Bridge Too Low

I once had a bit of an altercation with a 14-foot bridge.

I was aware that the controlling height throughout the entire inland waterway system was 15.5 feet, subject to variations in seasonal water levels. Higher than that and something had to come off or come down. Antennas, biminis, radar domes, and even flying bridges must sometimes be dismantled to permit passage. Some boats have been known to flood their bilges to sink into the water and bring their air height down. *Dart*'s mini-mast had permitted me to pass unhindered throughout the U.S. and Canadian waterways so far. The bridge ahead of me on the Trent-Severn was listed on the chart at 14 feet but will open if you are patient. Boating neighbors of mine told of a half-hour wait for the bridge to be opened. With a tide running, it's a long time to hold a small sailboat in midstream.

As I approached, I noted that the bridge was under some sort of reconstruction. A number of young, hard-hatted guys in jeans with sturdy leather tool belts, rugged boots, and impressive physiques were strung along the iron struts. They glanced toward me with apprehension, I thought. Maybe I was being overly sensitive, but I suspected they were thinking to themselves, watch out, woman driver, no spring chicken either.

I looked up at the tip of *Dart*'s mini-mast; I'd never actually measured the height, but eyeing it I'd have said it was less than 14 feet. I was sure I could make it under the bridge. *Dart* had about 10 feet to go when the workmen, as if choreographed, stopped work and craned over in unison to watch, and I had a sudden sinking feeling that I had miscalculated.

I flung the outboard engine into reverse, but it was too late. The propeller revved and churned the river water into greenish foam, but *Dart* is heavy, carries a lot of way, and the tidal flow was urging us on. I gritted my teeth as we slid ignominiously under the bridge with a horrid scraping, bumping, jolting, and finally a loud bang. The red-painted mini-mast toppled back gently onto the bimini frame and balanced there. I was out from under the bridge in only seconds and decided to pretend that I had planned the whole exercise. I had just released my patented, automatic, detachable fore-stay.

I steamed on upriver, blushing, not daring to look back, not betraying my dismay by a flicker until I was around a bend and out of sight. A small outboard boat with a family on board swung alongside.

"Are you all right?" Dad called out.

I laughed. "Well," I replied, "a bit surprised, but otherwise fine. Thanks for checking."

I cut the engine back to idle, left Wraith at the helm, and went forward to tidy up the rigging and secure the mast. I laid it forward onto the lifelines and lashed it into position. Then I steamed on up the river feeling somewhat chagrined. Once the broken forestay was repaired and replaced, I measured *Dart*'s mast-tip height above water level: 13.5 feet.

Must have been one of those seasonal water level variables.

*       *       *

The big dipper glowed and twinkled above me through the open fore hatch. The mosquito net blurred the familiar constellation, but within Dart's snug cabin, I was surrounded by planets.

Holst's famous suite played forth from the boat radio and filled the cozy interior with the musical themes of war, peace, winged messengers, and mystical eternity.

*Dart* was moored in a secluded park near a lock. The guide book noted that it was "isolated" with "no facilities for 15 miles," and I was aware of this as the daylight dwindled and the fishermen wound in their lines, closed up their tackle boxes, and left for home in their station-wagons. Finally, the lockkeeper drove off on his Honda Gold Wing motorcycle with a vanishing roar.

The trees draped themselves closely over the edge of the still, dark water and peered at their dim reflections. A groundhog shuffled through the undergrowth, and a chipmunk squeaked and chirped his way up a black willow tree. The evening parade of night herons took up their regimented stance and kept a sentinel watch on the frogs and snails and small fish in the shallows.

*Dart was moored in a secluded park near a lock.*

Public radio, my favorite evening choice, had announced the advent of an old favorite, Gustav Holst's "Planets Suite," and I planned my evening accordingly. By dusk, a supper of omelet, bacon, and fried tomatoes was dispatched; the dishes washed and stacked away; the final mouthfuls of chardonnay drained. The hush intensified. The shadowed night approached, eclipsing the magical pigments of the twilight sky, doubled in the still, smooth water. The peach and melon and rose faded to a vintage grey. Venus, the evening star, glowed watchfully.

Mars established his presence within the cabin, and while the dissonance of conflict rolled from the speakers, I closed up the boat. The washboards were dropped into position; the main hatch pulled closed; and for once—and I don't know why—I slid up the bolt that secures the hatch from within. Tucker and I climbed into our berth to the calming strains of Venus, the bringer of Peace, and I relaxed. The French horns and lush strings unwound me, and I pulled up the quilt around us and plumped up the feather pillows. Mercury, the winged messenger, provided energy and thrust, and I was now able to gaze upwards through the hatch into the clear night sky and pinpoint the familiar stars of the Big Dipper—Ursa Major, the Great Bear, the Plough. Fugitive slaves before the Civil War knew it as "the drinking gourd" and used the signpost in the sky to head north to the safety of Canada, following the two stars that form the side of the bowl that point to Polaris, the North Star.

Jupiter brought jollity and segued into the familiar theme that has also been set as a hymn: "I vow to thee my country," now given extra poignancy since it was sung at Princess Diana's funeral. Saturn, Holst's favorite, the bringer of Old Age, sounded the bell now clear and now distant, chiming the passing of the years. As the choir and orchestra faded into the vastness of eternity with Neptune the Mystic, Tucker and I dropped off to sleep.

It must have been a small, witching hour when I heard voices, voices of a group or gang of young men, rough and loud and chortling. My hackles rose, my throat went dry, my muscles tensed, and I thought to myself, "This could mean trouble." The thud of heavy boots, raucous laughter, and meaty hands slapping on muscular thighs. "Yes, this could really mean trouble."

Then I woke up.

The hush enveloped me and calmed my racing heart. The loudest noises were the pounding of my own pulse in my ears and the soft ticking of the brass ship's clock. Tucker, curled up beside me, dreamed on, making little woofing noises.

The boat was immobile, the silence profound. No boys, no troublemakers, no gang of youth bent on mischief. I lay quietly and reflected. This dream was a sign. My subconscious, my feminine intuition, Little Miss Ego, was sending me a message. I was aware when I came into the lock that it was isolated and secluded. I had bolted myself into the cabin. I had intended to stay below the lock where there were houses, a park, and children playing, but because the lockkeeper opened the gates for me, I felt compelled to motor through and away from the friendly atmosphere.

I should have heeded Little Miss Ego, who was constantly on the alert.

The night of the hateful knife attack, I had ignored her. She prodded me that night as I was about to doze off and warned me, "You haven't locked the back door." I told her sleepily to chill out and not bug me with silly notions... to my sustained regret. The intruder had opened the back door and walked right in.

Here was a new message, and I intended to listen up. From then on I was more careful where I tied up for the night.

# CHAPTER TWENTY-ONE

# The Big Chute!

"We'll take the small sailboat next—front and center!"

The authoritative voice crackled crisply from the loudspeaker across the sheltered basin in the Severn River where *Dart* and I were preparing to take the 60-foot plunge to Gloucester Pool.

I gulped nervously. We were about to ride the "Big Chute," a huge marine railway that hoists craft out of the Upper Severn River and conveys them down a steep hillside into Little Chute channel en route to Georgian Bay. The guidebook warned me to have plenty of lines ready to hand up to the staff who operate the machine. I had lines for every possibility attached port, starboard, bow, and stern. *Dart* looked as if she had just brushed through a giant spider web. Six fat fenders adorned each side of the small sailboat, and I felt she, and I, were ready for anything.

As I pushed the outboard engine into forward gear and steered between the towering steel sides of the giant travel-lift, the chief operator called down, "No need for lines, just keep her in gear until we tell you."

I thought I was going to steam right out the far side, but at the last minute the efficient operator pushed some buttons on his electric panel and a sturdy canvas sling slid up under *Dart*'s bow and snared her safely. A second sling raised up under her stern underbody, and we were ready to ride. A huge three-story cabin cruiser was called in behind me, and it loomed over my stern. I had the front row seat as the vast piece of machinery lumbered into motion, and I felt like minor royalty as tourists snapped our photograph and waved cheerily. I hoped they weren't waving farewell.

We hauled up out of the Severn River, water splashing down behind us, and now both boats were suspended mid-air, some 10 feet above ground. Traffic stopped on the rural road ahead of us as the lights turned to red, and we rumbled across in front of the stationary cars. Then the carriage stopped momentarily, and we swayed in the slings. The drop down the hill ahead of me was so steep I couldn't see the water below and for a moment visualized *Dart* slipping out of the slings and gliding insanely down the marine railway lines to plunge into the bay below. I need not have been concerned. The legs on the enormous carriage ingeniously adjust to the angle of the hill so the boats stay level. Whew!

*The giant mechanism was drawn, like some huge troglodyte, across the road.*

I relaxed enough to enjoy the changing scenery as we glided majestically downhill. The rolling farmland and wooded river banks had, over the past days, been gradually giving way to the smooth, pink, glacial boulders of the Canadian shield, with sturdy pines clinging onto small rocky islands. I had docked earlier that day, tied up *Dart* well out of the way, and walked along to watch the operation of the "chute." I joined an enthusiastic crowd of spectators for the fascinating sight. We all rushed to the road when the traffic lights turned red to watch in awe as the giant mechanism was drawn like some huge troglodyte by heavy steel cables across the road to descend the steep hill to Georgian Bay.

It was only three weeks earlier that I had turned *Dart* out of the wide-open waters of the Bay of Quinte on Lake Ontario and into the sheltered Trent-Severn waterway. Now the chute had transported me vertically into a whole new realm—the Georgian Bay.

*The channel was now bordered by smooth granite rocks supporting only the sturdiest of pine trees.*

*Dart* and I swung casually along a curvaceous channel, left, right, left, round the bends, carefully avoiding barren rocks and smooth, rocky islets, in a convoy of boats that had just exited Port Severn lock, the final lock on the Trent-Severn Waterway. Four of us left the lock together, and I pulled aside to let the faster boats pass. Following the leaders enabled me to enjoy the new scenery. We had crossed the frontier into Georgian Bay. Gone were the bosky woods, fallow fields, small towns, and narrow waterways of the Trent-Severn. The channel was now bordered by smooth, granite rocks, shaped by the glacier that ground its way through the area 20,000 years ago. The thin layer of soil remaining only supported the sturdiest of pine trees that huddled together, hunched over and braced against the prevailing winter winds.

Some islands sprouted a small cabin or two and rustic wooden docks; others resembled humpbacked whales about to surface and spout. One red-painted warning sign I passed advised "Sunken Island—Keep Clear." I wondered how it came to sink—or was this just a colorful analogy?

I was so busy spectating, it came as a shock when the pack leaders, coming to the end of the winding channel and 10 mph speed limit, suddenly opened their throttles, shot off in a cloud of spray and disappeared across Georgian Bay. The Bay! It's huge! Where is the next marker? Where am I?

I reeled back in horror and culture shock. I felt like Lawrence of Arabia gazing across the desert from a camel-top perch. The bleak mounds of islands behind me resembled a mirage of swelling sand dunes dotted with stunted, sun-dried bushes. I throttled back and pulled out the chart book. We had taken so many meandering curves on the twisting channel, I turned the chart this way and that and could not figure where I was or which way to go. Out in the Bay and half a mile ahead of me, I spotted a sailboat, mast lashed down on deck, motoring at a reasonable pace.

I pulled out my air horn and blew a short blast. The owners turned, and I waved. They stopped and waited for me to catch up.

"Where are you headed?" I called.

"Midland. How about you?"

"Wherever you're going. I'm going to follow you."

I hadn't planned to head straight to Midland, but with acres of smooth, cobalt blue, featureless water stretching for miles horizon to horizon, I thought it an excellent choice.

The sun was high and reflected off the glossy Bay surface, creating a white, refracted light that called for peaked cap and polarized sunglasses. The two sailboats proceeded at a leisurely pace, and as I relaxed and studied the chart, landmarks became clear. Fast sport cruisers, sightseeing boats, and ferries led the way deep into the Bay toward the town of Midland.

The coast approached, and I spotted features I could identify. I recognized from my guidebook the huge grain elevators decorated with the giant mural of the history of Midland. By the time my sailboat guides turned off, I was confident I could find my way to the municipal marina tucked in beyond piles of quarried stone awaiting shipment.

The breeze picked up, and I knew from the position of the marina that docking would be an awkward maneuver. I had to make a sharp left-hand turn to enter a pier with the wind now pushing me from behind and away from the dock. A friendly dad and his two small girls were quick to lend a hand. Kailey and Megan, despite their diminutive size, proved to be swift and competent by gripping *Dart*'s bow pulpit and hanging on firmly while dad grabbed a line and secured it 'round a cleat.

I invited the girls on board and awarded them Bermuda lapel pins for their kindness. They mused over the bag of pins for some time, selecting one then another. Kailey liked the little pink Bermuda cottage, and Megan preferred the elegant white Bermuda longtail bird. Ten minutes later, a choice made, Kailey was wearing the longtail and Megan the cottage.

The August sun baked the downtown marina, so cool showers and refreshing ice cream were welcome diversions. That evening I planned to celebrate with a delicious curry dinner, but when it came time to plug in ashore, I realized *Dart*'s power line would not reach the outlet unless I turned her completely around at her narrow pier. On the flashy speedboat alongside were four beer-drinking buddies partying merrily, music thumping. As they noticed my dilemma, suddenly *Dart* was taken in hand by a team of willing chaps who swarmed on board, handled lines efficiently, and in minutes she was repositioned, and my electricity was hooked up.

"I'd invite you for dinner," I called out, "but it would be thin pickings!"

"Don't worry, ma'am," came the jovial response. "We're well-stocked—with beer!"

# CHAPTER TWENTY-TWO

## The White Witch of the Marina

Tucker and I were comfortably settled in an expansive marina within several acres of wild scrub on the edge of Georgian Bay. It was good to be ashore for a while, firmly secured to an immovable dock, no poring over charts, no wondering where the heck we were.

Our surroundings at first appeared to be mundane scrub but on closer inspection revealed a mass of delightful blooms of all colors. At first, I wandered aimlessly, stepping over abandoned boat trailers, ducking under large sailboats perched on storage frames, and digging in vain into deep memory for the names of familiar blossoms. I gave up eventually and trekked off to my favorite cyber-bookstore, the Cottage Book Shop, and purchased Linda Kershaw's *Ontario Wild Flowers*.

Walks with Tucker became nature rambles, Tucker straining at the leash and I, head down, mumbling and exclaiming as I alighted upon a fresh specimen.

"Butter and eggs," I cried to Tucker in excitement. She rushed over and examined with me the diminutive plants with the tiny, yellow snapdragon blooms.

"Aren't they adorable!" I cooed.

She looked dubious. The color of the blossoms was exactly butter and eggs. But how could such a precious little plant be called toadflax, a member of the figwort family? In Scandinavia (I read) these same plants are boiled in milk to make an insecticide.

The wild sweet peas sent their crisp, sweet perfume to entice me, and I often brought a handful back to the boat. The delicate pink and mauve blossoms flung nets of colorful growth across rocky banks and grassy slopes. They originally escaped from gardens and turned wild along with the similar beach pea. But beach pea if eaten in quantity can cause paralysis.

The lovely lavender-blue bird vetch sprawled across the terrain, bees and butterflies enjoying the nectar-rich flowers. You can eat the young pods and seeds but must boil them first to destroy their toxins. A swath of golden blooms was flung across the grass, bird's foot trefoil in abundance. Tucker loved to race across the saffron-tinted lawn to the small, lakeside beach for swims and fetch-the-stick time. This cheerful, canary-colored wild flower was brought to North America for fodder and honey but fell out of favor, perhaps because the raw leaves and flowers contain cyanide.

*Wild flowers decorated* Dart*'s cabin following one of our nature rambles.*

Ah, the violet blue of alfalfa. I remembered this was a valuable fodder plant, and even today the sprouts are used in salads and sandwiches. But, warned my guide, alfalfa should be consumed in moderation as it contains substances that may affect liver function.

Wandering down a meandering, muddy track leading away from the marina, I spotted knapweed and learned that it is a permanent member of the top 10 list for noxious weeds. It's invasive, and since each plant can produce 20,000 seeds, it quickly outstrips the competition and once established gives off chemicals to prevent other plants from growing nearby.

The delightful blue stars scattered across the field proved to be chicory, sometimes grown as a commercial source of fructose. I was assured that the florets may be tossed in salad and the roots, dried, roasted, and ground, make a substitute coffee-like beverage. I recalled my mother and grandmother during the post-war years in England complaining about the acrid flavor of "chicory coffee."

Still exploring and searching, we came across a collection of derelict buildings, antiquated work sheds surrounded with discarded engines and rusting tools. Here grew in abundance what I had dismissed as unusually tall dandelions. They turned out to be prickly lettuce. The vertical upper leaves are said to align north-south. That could be useful, I mused, should I lose my way in the deep woods. And the bitter latex sap once dried can be used as a mild sedative.

We crunched our way to the edge of the large, gravel parking lot and plunged into the tall grass. So many of the yellow plants looked similar: hairy cat's ear, yellow hawkweed, perennial sow-thistle, goat's beard, all with comparable golden flower-heads.

The tiny white daisies were not daisies at all but scentless chamomile, described as a noxious, aggressive invader of pastures and hayfields, not to be confused with its cousin, stinking chamomile, readily distinguished by its foul smell.

"Ah, tansy," I alerted Tucker.

Busy with the scent of a wild rabbit, she was not interested in the tall, deep-yellow clusters of tansy blossoms, yet another "troublesome weed," traditionally used, I read, to repel lice and fleas, kill intestinal worms, and induce abortion. But it is also used to flavor cakes and puddings. The lovely little bracts of white florets turned out to be common yarrow, used to stimulate sweating, reduce inflammation, and stop bleeding. In addition, smoke from burning yarrow flowers will keep witches at bay.

We pushed our way through a dank, squishy reed bed to investigate the tall, fuzzy pinkish-purple plants which turned out to be spotted joe-pye weed. I never heard of them before, but it sounded useful. The root has been used in the treatment of diabetes, rheumatism, and persistent kidney and bladder problems.

What I mistook as wild parsley turned out to be the regal Queen Anne's lace, described as the great-grandmother of the domestic carrot. I didn't experiment, but apparently the first year roots of the young plants smell and taste like garden carrots. A number of the tall, slender plants with umbrella clusters of minute white blooms looked similar, but what a difference. The nutty-flavored roots of the common water parsnip could be harvested and eaten raw or cooked, but the almost identical spotted water-hemlock is so poisonous a single root can kill a horse. Children have apparently been poisoned by using pea-shooters made from dried water hemlock stems.

My brothers and I made peashooters as kids, but I guess they weren't hemlock. We fired unripe red currants from my stepfather's vegetable patch. You could fill your mouth with a whole battery and fire a rapid salvo very effectively.

Our walks passed in delightful contemplation. I fear that my boating neighbors eyed me askance as I wandered, nose in book, muttering apparent incantations to myself "...viper's bugloss, swamp vervain, deadly nightshade, great mullein, purple loosestrife, St. John's-wort, bladder campion, sulphur cinquefoil..." I reckoned after two weeks in Bay Port Marina I definitely qualified as a white witch.

*Tucker peering in from the deck.*

# CHAPTER TWENTY-THREE

# Not Too Close to the Falls

I gazed anxiously up at *Dart,* suspended some feet above me on a huge trailer. I needn't have been concerned. The driver, Doug Balsdon, had meticulously chained, lashed, tied, and roped her into position for the transfer from Georgian Bay to Buffalo, New York.

*Tim had driven from New Jersey to spend time with me.*

My cruising friend Tim had driven from New Jersey to join me, and we spent a delightful few weeks exploring Honey Harbor, camping on Beau Soleil Island, and touring through misty Parry Sound. The car was a definite bonus, and we set off by road for Niagara Falls and Kagawong on Manitoulin Island.

I had met Tim when he sailed, single-handed, into Bermuda the previous year on his small sloop *Varuna*. We spent time together, and after he sailed back to the U.S., we kept in touch. He was relaxing to be with. He didn't try and wrest the tiller from me or question my course or re-tie up the boat. I liked his favorite phrase, "Not making a suggestion, just thinking aloud, but how about we..." Who could resist such diffidence?

I recalled a rough, rainy day as *Dart* ploughed her way back toward Midland, Tim and I dressed head to toe in foul-weather gear, peering ahead through rain and spray, when he remarked in his affable manner, "I say, Gill, are those rocks ahead?" They were indeed, and a glance at the chart showed that I was definitely off course. It was a case when four eyes were better than two—with no recriminations!

Georgian Bay marked an important juncture for me. I had to consider whether *Dart* and I were capable of completing the Great Loop, a circular track back to New York via Lake Michigan, the TennTom Waterway, the Mississippi, the Gulf of Mexico, Florida, and the East Coast. Looking at the atlas back home, in the comfort and security of my own sitting room, it had seemed a real possibility. Reality had proved that each day does not run smoothly, according to plan, or even on schedule.

I was terribly torn. The Loop was a huge challenge. On the other hand, I hadn't reached Greece yet! That had been the real target for this year. I decided to turn back. *Dart* was just a tad too small, her outboard engine a fraction too under powered, or was it my nerve that failed? Perhaps so. But the Great Loop was not in the cards for this year.

Having made the decision against the Loop, it was time to turn south, and the shortcut via road would save me either a voyage back through the Trent-Severn or the long way round via Lakes Huron and Erie, a trip probably beyond my capabilities. I thought briefly of having the trailer take me to the head of the Hudson but chided myself for my lack of confidence.

"Keep the faith," I urged myself. "Remember, Greece, here we come."

Greece was indeed high on the list of priorities—not just high but at the top of the list. That was, after all, what this voyage was all about. I had been given a second chance at achieving a lifetime dream. How could I consider, even for a moment, not completing this venture? All right, it wasn't the real Greece—the wine dark sea, the Cyclades, the Ionian, the Aegean—and I wouldn't be negotiating the Gulf of Corinth with a mouth full of olives, but, over years, plans had to be modified and a new mission established. I'd had a dream and a sign, and, by golly, I was off to Greece, New York.

*We occasionally caught a glimpse of the trailer with its small but precious load.*

As we drove south in Tim's car with Tucker napping in the back seat, we occasionally caught a glimpse of the huge trailer with its small but precious load. Tim and I successfully negotiated our way through U.S. customs and immigration and held our breath as we watched the trailer inch its way forward in the heavy truck queue. But the trailer was pulled aside, and in the pouring rain, we splashed anxiously across the forecourt of the immigration buildings and joined the driver in the customs office. The young lady customs officer proved to be helpful and considerate, and when she learned of my voyage, she wanted to hear all about it. Then we were waved through and gratefully carried on to Tonawanda Island where *Dart* was deposited, ever so briefly, into the Niagara River.

Tim headed off home to New Jersey, and the next morning the marina staff saw me off with strict instructions, leaning over the edge of the dock, peering down and pointing firmly.

"Go straight across the river. See that sign right there? It says, Erie Canal entrance. Go straight there. Don't go down the river. Remember the Falls!"

Dart *was deposited, ever so briefly, into the Niagara River.*

With visions of Niagara Falls still fresh in my mind, I was only too happy to obey, and the three minute drama of cruising the Niagara River became a memory as *Dart* and I plunged into the green shade of the Tonawanda River and, beyond, the Erie Canal. Ahead of me lay 360 miles of sheltered waterway, ploughing a route right through the historic heart of America. I had already voyaged the eastern section of the canal from Waterford to Oswego and was intrigued to be traveling the western half in the opposite direction and discovering new places to visit.

It was only 180 years earlier that the canal was officially opened and the canal boat *Seneca Chief* set off from Buffalo for the initial journey through "Clinton's Ditch" as the canal was named, in honor of New York Governor Dewitt Clinton. The Erie Canal was an immediate success, showed a profit in 10 years, and was soon enlarged to cope with the large amount of marine traffic. The third and final enlargement, the Erie Barge Canal, was finished in 1918, incorporating canalized natural waterways such as the Mohawk and Seneca Rivers.

Now the canal's main focus is on recreational cruisers like *Dart*.

\*　　　　　　　　\*　　　　　　　　\*

STOP ! Wait for Green Light.

"Oh, shoot, I can't stop here," I thought.

There was a devilish current hurtling *Dart* fatefully toward the towering iron bridge that lay just ahead. "Blasted red light," I muttered as I flung the engine into reverse at full power. We were approaching Lockport, and I was nervous enough about the two huge locks that lay ahead. A closed bridge I did not need. The canal walls on both sides of us were steep, weed strewn, wet, dank, and offered no sign of bollards or cleats or so much as a wooden stake to hang onto.

Rain had set in, and I was hampered by my capacious but unwieldy rain jacket.

We began to swing sideways across the canal at an awkward angle, and the current was now pushing *Dart* swiftly, almost backwards, toward the looming concrete wall. The outboard engine and propeller fought courageously against the tide, but to gain steerage, I now had to shove the gear into forward. I spotted a huge white plastic drain pipe running vertically down the side of the canal wall. I managed to halt *Dart* alongside momentarily, and, by flinging both arms wide, I was just able to flick a line round the back of the pipe and with relief secured it to a cleat on deck.

*Dart* sat at an awkward angle with the current swilling past, but she had plenty of fenders between her and the rough stone wall, and we were secure enough for now. Phew!

I called the lockkeeper on the VHF radio and explained why I had made such a precipitate stop.

"Now that I'm tied up, I'm going to stay here for lunch," I advised him.

"That's fine," he assured me. "When you're ready, we'll open up the bridge, and there's just room for one small boat behind the lock wall if you want to tie up."

I trusted his judgment, but it was with trepidation that *Dart* and I crept forward into the tiny cut right alongside the lock. Sure enough, a space just big enough to tuck *Dart* in front of a rental canal boat. The canal boat left shortly afterwards, and I turned *Dart* around on her long lines so that she was now pointing outward and ready for a speedy departure should one be called for.

I docked *Dart* rather like an astute gunslinger prefers to sit in a bar, always facing the door, ready for a quick getaway or to reach for a gun. (I learned that when I was seven watching the Saturday morning cowboy movies.)

Dave, the lockmaster, stopped by for a visit with an impressive camera and asked to photograph *Dart* and her crew of two.

"I'm shooting stereo slides and compiling a show on locks," he explained. I was pleased to think that I had been recorded for posterity in stereoscopic mode. Under Dave's efficient management, *Dart* and I managed the two 25-foot locks the next day and set off cheerfully on a clear, sunny morning.

We didn't get very far.

Ahead lay one of the 15 lift bridges on the Erie Canal. The light was green, and *Dart* was already feeling the current behind her when the bridge was thankfully raised, but stopped half way. This proved to be a repeat maneuver of the previous day, and I was getting lots of practice at stopping—or trying to stop—and reversing in a tideway.

"Better tie up, we've got problems," the bridgekeeper advised me via radio.

The road running alongside the canal had stout steel rails abutting the waters edge. I managed to negotiate *Dart* alongside the road, which was close enough to reach with some dock lines. I walked Tucker along to the bridge house and chatted with the operator and technicians who told me the problem seemed to be electrical. Two hours passed, lunchtime approached, and I called

Dave up at the lock behind me to see if there was still space available above the lock.

"Just come back up; it's all clear," he advised me on the radio.

It was easy to turn *Dart* around by letting loose the stern lines and holding onto her bow pulpit while the current swung her stern right around. I jumped on board and had just pushed off heading back to the lock when the bridge bell rang merrily behind me, and looking around I saw the green light was on and bridge going up. I managed to turn *Dart* round again, and we headed through the bridge waving farewell to the now jovial bridgekeeper.

# CHAPTER TWENTY-FOUR

# Living With a Grin

We stopped at Knowlesville for a cup of afternoon tea and ended up staying for the night. A lift bridge lay across the canal and was ready to open on request to permit *Dart*'s passage, but I was ready to break for tea.

It was a tiny village, just a few quiet houses set back from the water's edge and a small general store. After I secured *Dart* alongside the rustic, stone dock, I put Tucker on her lead and walked over to the store. I bought a cold beer, a can of baked beans, and five stamps for postcards and settled in for a peaceful evening.

Mourning doves called poignantly from the trees beside us, and swallows dipped and swung across the placid water, chasing down dinner-on-the-wing. The canal curved through farmlands, vast meadows of rustling wheat, stands of ripening corn, and fields of lush green soya. Tucker had a wonderful romp along the towpath and then sat contentedly on the dockside beside *Dart*. Rachmaninoff's Piano Concerto spilled from the cabin radio, and I put down my book and enjoyed the music.

The evening sunlight glanced across the water and reflected up under the sycamore trees, giving the leaves a soft, dappled light that swayed in time with the music. A dragonfly rested briefly beside me. Dragonflies rode on the boat every day, mostly in pairs. They were iridescent blue and green and aqua. They rested and courted and took wing to make room for the next few pairs, sometimes half a dozen at a time. Occasionally, they shared traveling space with a migrating Monarch butterfly.

What fortune brought me to Knowlesville for this tranquil and evocative evening?

I wrote in a letter to my mother: "I am so happy, I live with a grin." It was a moment of total contentment. I was on board my beloved boat with my dear little dog/companion, and we were, together, pursuing a dream I had nursed for years.

*It was a cool, hazy morning.*

A calm, quiet night turned into a cool, hazy morning. The early sun illuminated the surface mist on the canal and the heavy dew on land. As Tucker and I walked the towpath, spiders had thrown gauzy cloaks across the shoreline banks of pink, granite stones. Others had woven tiny intricate nets within shoots of young reeds. Thrushes and robins bobbed along the path ahead of us, doves took flight in a clatter of wings as we approached, and a red-winged blackbird called out an anxious warning. A clanging of bells and the barricades on the road nearby were lowered for the first bridge raising of the day.

A pontoon boat with a family of Amish powered by with merry waves. The two men were sporting bushy beards, one black and one grey, and the women, their hair covered modestly, were in long sleeved, full skirted, cotton dresses. Young daughters were wearing demure frocks with long skirts. Two Amish teenagers cycled by on the opposite bank, attempting to keep pace with the boat. She was in a long, blue dress and white cap, he in white shirt, long dark pants, suspenders, and broad-brimmed hat. They, too, waved cheerily.

*Tucker stayed near two fishermen, kindred in their focus and attention.*

Two gruff old gents set up fishing camp on the dockside near the stern of the boat. Tucker happily joined them, and all three gazed intently and with happy anticipation at the slender nylon lines hanging slack in the canal. A small fish was reeled in and tossed to Tucker. She'd spent months watching and hoping for a real live fish, but now that she had one, she was not sure what to do with it. She mouthed it cautiously. It was cold, wet, and wriggly. The fisherman laughed and tossed it back into the canal. I photographed Tucker and the two fishermen, strangely kindred in their focus and attention.

I had started shooting slides as well as prints. My techie friends assured me I should be shooting in digital, but I guess I was old-fashioned enough to enjoy the heft and balance of my Olympus OM 2000 with zoom lens. Solid and dependable though it was, the manual controls were a distinct disadvantage for the "snap" shot. One morning I noticed a tall, brown figure lurking at the side of the canal, partly concealed in the bushes. As *Dart* motored past, I saw it was a deer. I had time to raise my camera but no chance to focus or adjust the exposure. The result seen on a 4"x6" print was barely recognizable. So my day-to-day camera remains my small, neat, gold Olympus Stylus, totally automatic and 100 percent reliable. All my best shots are taken with what some might dismiss as a pocket camera. It hangs right at hand near the cockpit, and I can snatch it up for a fast shot at a moving target.

I rarely shoot in monochrome though it is my real preference. Color seems so banal at times, so predictable; monochrome shows the substance, the shadow, the symmetry, and the harmony without the confusion of hue.

My photographic career began at the age of eight when my grandfather gave me a "box Brownie" camera and a developing kit. I became adept at processing rolls of film in little open trays of chemicals in a darkened attic with a dim, red lamp. Prints were produced in a small frame, exposed to sunshine before I rushed back up the steep ladder to the loft to soak the small sheets of paper in developer and watch the captured scene unfold. There was mother hanging my baby brother's cloth nappies on the laundry line; our large black dog, Gunner, tongue hanging loose; and the rear view of our house, beds of pansies in the foreground, slightly blurred.

Little did Grandpa imagine that his gift would lead to an engrossing lifelong hobby and eventual career as a newspaper photographer, reporter, and feature writer in England and later in Bermuda.

# CHAPTER TWENTY-FIVE

# Welcome to Greece!

"Welcome to Greece."
I gave a great shout of delight.
"Greece!"
"Tucker, we're here, this is it, this is Greece—at last."
Tucker leaped up into the cockpit from the cozy berth where she had been napping. She looked disheveled and bewildered, one ear bent upward at an odd angle.

*"Tucker, we're here, this is it, Greece—at last!"*

The canal bank was constructed of boulders and impossible to tie up against, so I carried on, still chirping to myself with excitement. About half a mile further along, I spotted a small wood dock about *Dart*'s size. I tied her up, and carrying two cameras and tugging Tucker along, I set off in haste back down the canal way trail to the sign. It was steamy and hot, and in my haste I forgot sunglasses and hat, but I was too thrilled to notice. Luckily, two girl joggers had stopped for a breather near the sign, and they gladly photographed my significant moment.

"Welcome to Greece." The large and elegant sign was right on the side of the Erie Canal as we steamed by. I pulled *Dart*'s engine out of gear and drifted along, admiring the wonderful green and white painted sign on its tall, wood stand. I couldn't have asked for better proof that my ambition had finally been realized. This was a moment dreamed of for 40 years—more than that actually, with modifications along the way. This important occasion had to be recorded for posterity and proof.

It was over 40 years ago that I had left my family and life in England and relocated to Bermuda, the better and faster to save funds to buy my own boat and sail to Greece! So it wasn't the Greece of my decades-old plan, but it was the Greece of the recent portentous dream that brought me here, and, by golly, I was going to relish the achievement.

*Tucker, my boat buddy, rain or shine.*

I hugged Tucker, buried my nose in her soft fur, thanked her for being with me, and assured her that without her, I could never have completed the journey. She'd been my boat buddy, my companion, my cuddle-bunny, my watchdog. She'd licked my tears, shared my meals, even helped wash the dishes. She had sat with me on *Dart*'s bow on calm, sunny days while Wraith steered, sheltered with me in the cozy cabin on rainy days, and snuggled with me on chilly nights. She had spent hours waiting patiently outside dress shops, bookstores, and supermarkets, and always greeted me with a warm and enthusiastic welcome. Together we had reached Greece.

\*     \*     \*

"I hear you make a great pot of beans!"

The unsolicited praise from a total stranger came as a complete surprise. Tucker and I were on an evening stroll around the canal-side village of Fairport when a congenial, mustached chap approached me with the inquiry, "Aren't you on the little sailboat?"

When I confirmed that was so, he offered me the unusual but genuine compliment, and when I looked intrigued, he added, "Your friends on the Gulfstar were here a couple of days ago and told me about your beans."

It had been about three nights previously when the only three boats docked at Holley held an impromptu potluck supper. Jim and Debbie, Amy and Peter, and Tucker and I loaded the dockside picnic table with a variety of dishes and tucked into a huge dinner of chicken, corn cobs, cole slaw, salad, and baked beans. My pot of beans had obviously proven memorable. I always keep a few cans of beans on board for just such occasions. Not having an oven, a pot of beans is an easy dish to prepare and carry to a social event. I fried up some chopped onions and bacon, stirred in dark brown sugar, mustard, seasonings, a dash of curry powder, a smidgen of Outerbridge Sherry Pepper sauce, then added the Bush's baked beans. A splash of black rum added extra zing.

Holley had proven to be an admirable stopping off point, offering excellent facilities and a short walk to a spacious supermarket. The entire town center was under reconstruction, but despite the chaos and noise, I could see it was going to be well worth the trouble. Tucker was even welcomed into the library.

"Oh, we have lots of members with dogs," the kindly librarian assured me. "You may certainly bring her in."

Tucker curled up happily on top of my backpack on the floor while I went on-line and checked e-mails.

*Tucker gazed at the huge flock of ducks in Pittsford.*

We had stopped for lunch at Pittsford where Tucker gazed entranced at the huge flock of ducks that hung about the public dock waiting for a handout. We shared an ice cream; then we carried on to Fairport, passing the intersection with the Genessee River. There had been so much rain recently, the runoff had turned the river to a rich brew of latte.

At Fairport, we tied up at a pleasant, wooden dock ahead of the famous main street lift bridge. Tom, the affable dockmaster, came by for a visit and advised me to move through the bridge and across the canal to the concrete dock where we would be closer to modern washroom facilities.

"The bridge is in Ripley's Believe It or Not," he advised me proudly. "It's the only bridge in the world built on a bias, and no two angles in the bridge are the same. It's an irregular decagon."

I was suitably impressed and paid due homage when the bells rang, the traffic was drawn to a halt, and the irregular decagon lifted to let *Dart* pass beneath.

It rained all night, and we arose late. After visits to the library and supermarket, I rented a pedal bike for an hour and took Tucker for a long run on the towpath. She loved it and went racing ahead of me at 20 knots or more. By the time we made the turn at the end of the first half-hour, she was slowing a bit, but she had really needed a good work out. (Actually, it was I who was slowing a bit.)

The boating life may appear to be a healthy life, but I didn't really find it so. There were hours of steering, standing at the helm, followed by one great leap ashore with dock lines, then weariness set in. Just being aboard kept the small muscles permanently on the move, maintaining balance and equilibrium. I lost weight on the move and gained it from the evening glasses of wine (strictly rationed to two and a half).

Sunscreen and moisturizer were essential applications, but I still attained a certain wind-swept, sunburned appearance that marked the long-term boater. Was it a badge of honor or a stigma? I was never quite sure. Are you on a boat? Was the question an insult or a compliment? I was never quite sure. But I recognized that my countenance told a tale or two.

That evening, a great swing band played in Kennelley Park across from the dockside, and visitors streamed in to visit the antique and classic car show that had gathered there. The villagers of Fairport describe themselves as "front porch friendly," and so it proved to be. We spent a couple of days there, walking the village streets lined with handsome Victorian buildings, gardens of petunias and snapdragons, and patriotic flags fluttering from amenable front porches.

# CHAPTER TWENTY-SIX

## Coast Guard Approved

"Three old ladies locked in the lavatory. Nobody knew they were there."

One of those silly ditties I sang as a child echoed in my mind in Seneca Falls where Tucker and I very nearly ended up locked in a lavatory.

The search for a toilet was a daily challenge. I didn't have a head on *Dart*; there really wasn't room. Later Flicka models jammed a toilet compartment into the tiny boat, but it takes up half of the full length settee/berth. I preferred to have the space on board even though it meant some interesting and sometimes urgent explorations on a daily basis. Tucker and I set out early in search of suitable facilities. I had become an expert at tracking down toilets. You could say I had developed quite a nose for the quest.

*The waterfront at Seneca Falls.*

Gas stations, for example, were always good for a toilet. I'd just buy a few groceries and ask for the key. Building sites provided a portajohn for their workmen. The rumble of payloaders and the churning of cement mixers was a good sign. The construction site loos were usually in a conspicuous place, but I toughened my inhibitions and just marched coolly in, tying Tucker to the door handle. I learned to act fast. No time to read the daily news.

One morning in Seneca Falls, home of the Women's Rights Movement, I walked along the waterfront and spotted the open doors of the Seneca Falls Historic Area Maintenance Department. The long workshop had several garage doors standing up and open and a few workmen in uniform bustling about.

I strolled casually up and inquired politely, "Do you have a bathroom I might use?"

"Sure do, Ma'am," came the friendly response, and I was shown into the rear of the white painted, brick building. Tucker and I had a spacious tiled bathroom to ourselves for a while, but as we made our exit, it was to find all but one of the rolling doors now tight shut, the guys all piled into work trucks outside, and the last door rumbling down. I quickly ducked underneath and gave a cheerful wave to the startled work team. I guess they forgot I was there.

I learned to use a toilet whenever I came across one, in libraries, church halls, restaurants, parks, and lockkeepers' offices. I spent one night moored in Newburgh on the town's extensive, renovated waterfront. They have a grand new toilet block, but it is locked at night and not opened until—well, who knows when, but too late for me.

Tucker and I set off early in the morning, walking along the colorful river front laid out with red brick walks; colorful flower beds of geraniums, petunias, and alyssum; and one restaurant after another. We came across a work team hosing out the back entrance of a beer hall after a busy Saturday night. They willingly allowed me access to the ladies room. I tiptoed through pools of water on the red tiled floor, beer cans swilling past, and food scraps and paper detritus being swept up.

In one small town on the Erie Canal, the spacious timber facility intended for visiting boaters was closed and undergoing major renovation to be ready for the following season. I spotted a short stepladder leaning against the building, providing access to some big, sliding doors standing ajar. Climbing up and peering into the workshop area, I noted the door to a hallway was held open with a chunk of wood. Investigating further, I found a row of super brand new tiled bathrooms and toilets in good working order. Watching out for workmen and discreetly nipping up the ladder became a daily event.

I did at one point have a porta-potti on board *Dart*, but it really got under foot.

Bucket-and-chuckit might work in mid-Atlantic, but the inland waterway authorities are extremely strict about the dumping of waste. I had a night jar for midnight pees, and for greater emergencies, had a locker full of what I called poop-bags. These are like one-time chemical toilets, jolly handy to have on board in a crisis although not particularly user friendly.

The U.S. Coast Guard officer who came on board *Dart* to give her a safety check was mostly concerned with emergency signaling equipment and preventing overboard disposal from marine toilets. He was surprised when I confessed to not having a head on board, and when I showed him a sample poop bag, he was startled. But he presented me with my qualifying green shield sticker, and I quickly slapped it onto *Dart*'s red mini-mast.

# CHAPTER TWENTY-SEVEN

# Elephants in the Garden

Elephants! Good grief!

The family of elephants standing in the riverside garden had their trunks raised as I motored past. I'd seen plenty of bogus deer, plastic geese, sham swans, a family of deceptive ducks, an impressive life-size bronze moose, concrete gnomes with funny red hats and noses, and false pink flamingos, but ersatz elephants—that showed imagination.

We were steaming along the Seneca River, farmland on one side with shorn meadows of mown hay and on the other side, a herd of black and white cows ruminating thoughtfully in fetlock-deep water. We passed Hickory Island, fields of corn ready to be picked since it was just about as high as an elephant's eye, ersatz or not.

We passed an enormous trailer park, every trailer with its own tiny wooden jetty with a sporty speed boat tied alongside. Some had built patios around their trailers with screened tents beside them, dining sets within, and impressive barbecues without. A huge crane with a boat sling was parked on the bank ready to pull every craft out of the water as winter approached.

Two thunderstorms with torrential rain had cooled the air. Early that morning, as I peered out through the lexan washboard, I saw a small, damp, heron perched disconsolately on the stern rail.

I set off to steam through the Montezuma Wildlife Reserve. The sides of the canal opened right up, revealing meadows of colorful wildflowers on both sides, with the occasional single giant oak tree. Black-eyed Susan and purple loosestrife provided a colorful contrast, but alas, the latter, although a cheerful accent, is considered a pernicious weed within wetlands, gobbling up the habitat of rare native species.

Swallows darted to and fro above me, a few Canada geese paddled in the shallows at the waters edge, and the ubiquitous belted kingfisher swooped ahead of me by a few yards. These seemed to have settled happily along the canal, and I met a new pair every half mile or so. They all acted the same, darting, diving, and squawking ahead of me as if to lead the way. Then they passed me along to the next pair who took over escort duty. They seem to have divvied up the canal bank amicably.

*A life-size bronze moose.*

There were tiny, buff-colored wading birds that skittered across the stones on the water's edge scampering ahead of *Dart*. They moved so fast I couldn't get a good look at them, even with the binoculars. The weather forecast was not good, but apart from a light shower earlier, it looked as if it was going to be a hot summer day. Wraith was steering the boat, so I was able to go forward and perch on the bow where I could enjoy the sound of the water chuckling as it rippled alongside the bow.

A large yellow fish leaped out of the water ahead, probably a bass, and I saw a mysterious grey humpbacked creature walking through the low undergrowth on the bank side. It looked like a wild hog rooting for truffles but turned out to be the arched back of a large blue heron walking head down searching for snacks in the shallows. It startled me for a minute, but I startled him. You'd think herons would be used to boats passing by, but no, they'd wait until the very last minute until the boat was abreast of them before they heaved themselves into the atmosphere, croaked angrily, and flapped resentfully away only to cross the canal and settle again.

An osprey flew close overhead. He carried in his claws a fish almost as big as himself.

We passed a huge commercial installation with vast factories and monster chimneys, derricks and pipes, and railways and silos. Nothing moved, no sounds of machinery or engines, no puffs of steam or smoke, not a soul about, and the enormous wharf alongside appeared virtually disused. Further down, a group of young children on a school outing were walking along the canal trail near a narrow road bridge. They carried sketch pads and notebooks and were excited to spot *Dart*. I called Tucker up from below, and as she sprang up into the cockpit, the kids called out excitedly,

"Hi! Hi ! What's her name? Hi, Tucker!"

They ran along the canal path for a short way, waving and calling, and we turned and waved back.

"'Bye, Tucker, 'bye Tucker," their voices drifted off into the distance.

Looking ahead down the clear, straight canal, I could see through three bridges, each doubled in the still water, and beyond them, misty hills in the distance. An inlet leading off to my right curved back onto itself in a loop. We passed a floating field of frail pink water lilies. Monet would have loved it.

# CHAPTER TWENTY-EIGHT

## The Bus to Penny Lane

"Did you know any of the Beatles?"

"Why, yes," I quipped. "John Lennon and I played together as kids. We were only four when we rode off on our tricycles to find the Strawberry Fields. Our Mums were furious. We were only in our knickers."

The widened eyes, dropped jaws, and incredulous looks from my small but attentive audience told me my quirky British humor had gone too far.

"Oh, I'm only kidding," I reassured my amazed listeners, gathered in the friendly little boat club on the shores of Lake Onondaga.

"But I did take the ferry 'cross the Mersey many times," I added, "and when I went to visit my Nana in Liverpool, I used to catch the Penny Lane bus."

It was strange but fun to find myself in Liverpool, N.Y., 62 years almost to the day after my birth in Liverpool, England. Not only was I in Liverpool, but in the warm and welcoming atmosphere of the Onondaga Yacht Club.

The visit occurred spontaneously toward the end of my second summer of cruising. I was feeling much braver—not reckless, but definitely adventurous enough to leave the prescribed course. When I spotted the town of Liverpool on the shores of Onondaga Lake, I was confident enough to swing off the Erie Canal and into the broad, smooth reach of the lake.

The lake shore was heavily wooded with impressive mansions set in clearings amid luscious lawns. Paths ran along the shoreline threading amongst husky trees, and I could see droves of walkers, joggers, and cyclists enjoying the afternoon sun. The entry marks to the town marina were tiny and hard to spot, but as I got closer to shore, I saw the red and green lights and turned in between them. I headed to the nearest empty dock space and tied *Dart* up. I was right alongside the local Yacht Club so I went over to ask permission to stay.

I discovered that I was at the visitors' pier of the town marina, not the club dock, but in the meantime I met several friendly members and received a pressing invitation to their pot luck supper that night. I prepared a large dish

145

of my famous baked beans and joined the informal party. After being introduced after supper, I was happy to regale them with tales of the voyages of *Dart*, her captain, and first mate, Tucker. Watching and listening to their reaction, the gasps of wonder, the chuckles and laughs, I gained a new estimation of myself, of the voyage, of *Dart*. I had been on my own for so long, I had no idea of my own accomplishment; I was too close to it, too involved in it, to form an opinion. The appreciative camaraderie of the small boat club gave me a new perspective of my own achievement. I began to feel good about myself! Even Little Miss Ego conceded that I had come this far without major setbacks.

After dinner, several of the lady members clambered onto *Dart* to gaze in amazement at the small, neat space in which we lived and traveled. During the next few days, affable club members drove me around the surrounding area as far as Syracuse and the famous university. They made sure that I visited Heyd's diner where the real Beatles had munched on hamburgers some years previously. I was loaned a bicycle, and on the cycle path, Tucker happily raced ahead of me at the end of her leash as I pedaled and strained to keep up; that is, until a park ranger stopped me to warn that a dog on lead must be walked, not driven like a husky in an Iditerod.

*Dart* was pressed into service as the committee boat for the Club's regatta.

*Dart* was pressed into service as committee boat for the Club Regatta, and she looked eye-catching and colorful decked out in every flag I had on board: yards of red, yellow, and blue bunting; my U.S. and Bermuda courtesy flags; my Chesapeake Bay Schooner Race flag; my SSCA flag; my AGLCA burgee; my Women Aboard flag; and, topping them all, my huge Gosling's Black Seal Bermuda rum flag. I felt I was truly a flagship for the day. But there was more to this small, delightful town than a friendly neighborhood and welcoming yacht club.

As I delved into the history of the area and learned about the Onondaga tribe, I discovered that I was within a truly significant heritage site.

That evening as I relaxed in the cockpit, sipped a glass of cold white wine, and watched the evening sky transmute from lemon to saffron to gold, I pondered the fate of the first nations. All that remained in the area were remnants of tribal possessions in museums and names that were scattered across my charts and maps.

I learned that the Onondaga (People of the Hills) were one of the founding six nations of the Iroquois Confederacy which included the Seneca, Cayuga, Oneida, Mohawk, and Tuscarora tribes. The original meeting was held on the north-east shore of Lake Onondaga over 400 years ago, and councils are still held there today not far from where I sat on *Dart*.

The names haunted me in the coming weeks as I voyaged through the Cayuga-Seneca canal, across Lake Oneida, and along the beautiful Mohawk River. With every turn of a chart book page, I was reminded of the indigenous inhabitants, the native Americans, who once inhabited these spacious lands and waterways and who were now reduced to labels on a chart.

# CHAPTER TWENTY-NINE

## Taken With a Pinch of Salt

"Have you visited the Salt Museum yet?" I was asked by one of my new friends in Liverpool.

I had seen the tall, strange wooden structure with the steep pitched roof at the end of the park trail and decided against a visit. What could possibly be interesting about salt, right? Then I reminded myself of my early promise to journey with knowledge and not in ignorance. The museum loomed beyond the marina, within sight of *Dart,* so I dutifully set out one morning, after walking Tucker and shutting her below in *Dart* with her breakfast snack. I found a whole new realm of knowledge.

I discovered the Onondaga Indians had long been aware of the local salt springs but found no use for the bitter water, believing it to be possessed by demons. They showed the springs to a visiting French Jesuit missionary, Father Simon LeMoyne, in 1654, and he recognized the value of the salty brine. He was there to arrange a peace treaty with the Iroquois Five Nations and also to establish a Jesuit mission. The establishment of a rudimentary salt trade was an unexpected bonus.

However, it wasn't until the late eighteenth century that the first permanent salt works was established in Onondaga County in what was designated "Salt Springs Reservation." In 1797, the salt springs were taken over by the State of New York to maintain quality control, prevent a monopoly, and provide revenue to the state. The early, crude, salt boiling "blocks" consisted of a row of about six, 60-gallon cauldrons of brine set over open fire pits and exposed to the weather. Later, more efficient blocks were enclosed within wood houses, and as many as 60 kettles were heated over flues running from a furnace to a chimney. Salt water pumped in from the spring through log pipes was brought to boil, and as salt crystals formed on the surface, they were removed with a long-handled scoop and set in woven ash baskets to drain. Blocks operated around the clock, employing two shifts as the kettles were boiled down two or three times every 24 hours. The lakeside Salt Museum has recreated a "boiling block" and incorporated the nineteenth century chimney that was once part of "Salt Block 56," erected by Stephen Van Alstine in 1856.

As I wandered through the open gallery of the museum, I noted the long stave-handled scoops, the woven baskets, and the huge iron cauldrons, all saved from the past. Wonderful old sepia photographs captured remarkable scenes of the boiling blocks where men labored in intense heat as they skimmed the newly formed salt crystals off the top of the boiling brine.

They wore knee-high boots, broad-brimmed hats, and trilbys or cloth caps; the head gear was universal and apparently essential. The coarse solar salt was shown being tipped by the half barrel into horse drawn carts for removal. Photographs showed teams of coopers who were kept busy year round producing barrels required for the shipment of the finer, boiled salt.

Eventually, the lack of wood and cost of importing coal led to the return to solar salt, an earlier and cheaper method of production. Between 1888 and 1926, solar salt became the predominant product of the Onondaga manufacturers. Sun and wind produced a coarse but economical commercial salt, but once again they were reliant on good weather.

The shallow evaporation pans or "aprons" containing the brine were open to the air but had movable covers that could be quickly pushed into place for shelter. At the peak of the solar salt industry, nearly 50,000 salt rooms or "covers" blanketed the Salt Springs Reservation. Warning bells were rung when rain threatened, and entire families were summoned, day or night, to assist in the critical protection of the precious salt. Children ran from school and parishioners from church when the alarm sounded.

Immigrant labor kept the boiling salt blocks operating. Prior to the Civil War, there were Irish, British, and German laborers; post-war, Italians, Poles, and Eastern Europeans worked 10 to 12 hours a day, often seven days a week from March to December. Solar workers had an easier life without the heat and danger of the boiling vats but were on call 24 hours a day, processing the salt and preserving it from inclement weather. Before other salt operations from the west coast and overseas forced the local manufacturers out of business, they were producing three to four million bushels of salt per year. Each bushel required between 30 and 60 barrels of brine.

The salt pans, buildings, and equipment were abandoned in the 1920s to crumble with disuse until the Great Depression when Governor Franklin Delano Roosevelt turned the state land over to Onondaga County. With funding through the Work Relief Bureau, the area was converted to the extensive, wonderful park that is much used today, and in 1933, the Salt

Museum, constructed from remaining timbers of old salt covers, was opened to the public.

*I felt very much at home in the town of Liverpool on Lake Onondaga.*

As I walked out of the museum and gazed across the strange briny lake, I found I had developed a new respect for salt. Never again would I take a pinch casually. I would always remember the strange, demonic, salt springs of Onondaga County.

# CHAPTER THIRTY

# Crumbs Along the Mohawk

Hurricane Isabel brought us to an unexpected halt. She was gyrating menacingly in the Atlantic but heading vaguely in the direction of New York, the Hudson River, and us.

I had joined a group of boaters traveling at a similar speed, and as we progressed along the Erie Canal, we became a sociable support team commiserating with each other over balky engines and equipment, sharing alfresco breakfasts, and ordering joint take-out pizza suppers.

We visited back and forth from one boat to another, steamed along at the same rate each day, and tied up in unison each evening.

Being used to the potential danger of hurricane weather, I announced that with Isabel heading anywhere even suspiciously in my direction, I would remain where I was. Waterford was not only sheltered, it was also one of my favorite waterside towns and housed a great little shop—Antiques and Uniques—where I regularly stocked up on unusual books. It proved a propitious decision, since only a couple of days later anxious boaters were streaming north up the Hudson River away from Isabel's potential swath of destruction. The coastal marinas quickly filled up, and the Waterway authority announced they would open the locks for any craft to take shelter within the canal.

We secured all our boats, checked each other's dock lines and fenders, and sat tight for a week. We hung out together, enjoying potluck suppers on the picnic tables at the Waterford Visitor Center, eating together in the Irish pubs, and taking long walks with Tucker along the canal-side trails. The local television news crew came and interviewed us and filmed our careful preparations for high winds. We gathered to watch ourselves on the evening news.

A group of us were enjoying coffee in a local diner one morning after a hike to the hardware store, and idly perusing the list of Stewart's ice cream flavors, when I spotted "Crumbs along the Mohawk." I pointed it out to the group.

*The local television news crew came and interviewed us.*

"That's what we should call ourselves, Crumbs along the Mohawk," I mused.

We chuckled at the possible interpretation of the name. Did it mean that the lead boat scattered a bread-crumb trail for the others to follow? Or did it refer to Janice's agreeable habit of making super, crunchy toast while underway, signaling *Dart* to come alongside *Ragged Chutes* and passing over slabs of crisp, hot, whole wheat toast liberally plastered with butter and marmalade?

We sampled the ice cream, caramel flavored with chunks of graham cracker and caramel swirl. It was very good, and it was for sale all along the Mohawk River that our group had recently traversed.

After 10 days in Waterford awaiting the passing of Isabel, the boats set off on different days and in various directions. Now it was time for me to check out of my sheltered marina and head south too. Grizzled, corpulent clouds loomed and prepared indifferently to spit into the chill wind from the south. I disconnected the power line, started the engine, and untied the dock lines from my marina pier. Tucker had sensibly dived below into a nest of quilts in the snug vee berth. I powered down the center of the long line of slips filled with bobbing and swaying craft of all sizes and types—small sailboats, fast power cruisers, and spacious floating homes.

We steamed out of the inlet and onto the cheerless Hudson River. The wind was dead on the nose, and an uncomfortable, sloppy swell rolled up the river. *Dart* was not at all happy. She reared and plunged hesitantly into the oncoming waves, then threw off a cloud of spray as each wave stopped her short for a minute. I thought to myself, I can't face a whole day of this. Fifteen minutes later, we were back in the same slip, power connected, kettle on the stove, and cable TV plugged in and switched on. Five minutes later came a patter of boisterous raindrops on the canvas bimini, and 10 minutes later, torrential rain cascaded, lightning honed the marina, tumultuous thunder snarled, and gusts of wet wind swirled through the moored boats. Thank heaven I came back in. First to the weather channel; it didn't sound good for the next day either.

My good friend Don picked me up for an expedition to Barnes and Noble's super bookstore and a nearby diner for a hearty breakfast of rich pancakes soaked in syrup and slathered with butter, a good sugar boost for the next day's voyage.

I was twitchy and anxious the next morning, so I was disconnected, untied, and on my way out of the marina by 6:45 a.m. Thank heaven the Hudson was mild and fairly calm. The wind had switched to the west, so I had a slight lee. I wondered how my group of boating buddies made out. Once Isabel had passed into history, they all set off. *Jenna Star* was heading down river, then north up the coast. *Ragged Chutes, Lunatic Fringe, Suvarov, Windswept,* and other sailboats were off to marinas to erect their masts for onward voyages. I reminisced as I steered *Dart* south down the Hudson.

The VHF radio was switched on, and I heard *Ragged Chutes* within radio distance, so I called for a chat. They were not far behind, all motoring in a loose pack, and now coming into sight as they caught up with the baby of the fleet. Just for once I was ahead of the troupe.

I had happily spent many months voyaging solo, but the previous weeks had shown me a different way of travel, as part of a team. I had stoutly maintained my independence while journeying alone, but traveling in company had provided its own pleasures and joys and a built-in support system. After a week apart, it was fun to head south together. We radio-chatted back and forth during the long day.

I knew *Dart* was making 5.2 knots, but the GPS showed our speed over the ground was 2.5 knots. What a tide! My band of boat-mates gradually pulled ahead of me; the Chesapeake Bay, Intracoastal Waterway, and

Bahamas lay in their cruising futures while I was heading for New Jersey where passage was booked for *Dart* on a Bermuda-bound freighter..

I called over the radio, "I'm saying good-bye now to the 'Crumbs along the Mohawk.' I wish you all safe voyages, quiet anchorages, and, most important of all, good friendships." The five tall masts ahead of me gradually faded into the mist on the horizon.

*The "Crumbs Along the Mohawk" enjoyed a Pirate Party.*

# CHAPTER THIRTY-ONE

# Homeward Bound

There was something quite compelling about being on the move on the waterways: *Dart*'s leisurely progress through the silken water; the way the golden reeds on the water's edge drifted past one depth of trees, delicate, emerald, sweeping willows and beeches which slid in front of another darker group of chestnuts and oaks. In the background loomed the hills, smoky and mauve and mysterious, and behind them the distant, enigmatic, mountain ranges.

*There was something compelling about being on the move.*

The clouds changed constantly, like scrambled smoke signals from a fickle tribe, and carried me from shade to shadow. I lived within the weather, standing in the open cockpit, just a small canvas cover between me and the wind, sun, and rain. I varied dress to accommodate the temperature, and the boat's movement forward created my own subtle, organic air-conditioning.

Every breath drew in the immediate atmosphere, and I felt enfolded in the ambience: early morning sun-warmed air; moist, afternoon fog; cold, crisp evening breezes; delicious, heavy fragrance from blossoming trees; rank, fleeting, farmyard odors; and the dank, elusive smell of the waterway—weed, wet wood, and damp stone.

I was aware, too, of the sound of the engine, all that stood between me and precarious immobility. I was conscious of the imperceptible ticking of the pistons and carburetor, and the water pump's slender stream of cooling water that splashed lightly into the river behind me. After an hour of proficient motoring, the sound of the engine settled into my subconscious to be guarded vigilantly. The slightest alteration in note or rhythm and I became instantly alert. Many factors altered the sound of the engine: the hood of my rain jacket pulled up or dropped back, a turn of head to left or right, the pressure of the rudder close to the propeller as I pushed the tiller, even a yawn, all modified the refrain of my sturdy little Yamaha outboard engine.

I loved feeling I was right in the heart of America, traveling at walking pace, tucked away, incognito.

"What hills are those?" I called out to a lockkeeper as we pulled away. I thought perhaps he'd tell me "the Appalachians," but he looked over his shoulder and advised me, "Big Nose and Little Nose."

A sudden, shocking roar and violent engine noise startled me from my reverie; a train raced urgently through the nearby coppice of slender beeches reverberating against the canal banks. I forgot until I studied the chart that the train tracks paralleled the waterway for many miles.

Occasionally, I was astonished to come upon a monstrous curve of concrete motorway that tilted its burden of racing vehicles up and over the peaceful waterway, then vanished in its race to the metropolis over the horizon. I once spotted the bizarre peak of a brightly colored ferris wheel looming above the oaks and pines, as unexpected as a crop circle in a field of turnips.

A dead tree on the edge of the river sported two mysterious, black, shaggy lumps within its sparse branches. As I motored past in *Dart,* the silhouetted spheres simultaneously raised gleaming, white heads; proud, hooked, yellow beaks; and dark glinting eyes from within their ruffled feathers—a pair of magnificent bald eagles.

It was a spectacular, crisp, sunny day when I ran south down the Hudson in *Dart*, the Catskills just perceptible in the distance through air as clear as a glass of Chablis. I left Wraith at the helm and perched on the bow drinking in the atmosphere. Tucker walked carefully along the narrow side deck to join me, and *Dart* created our own soft breeze as we jogged forward at a relaxed pace.

A distant honking drew my attention upward, and I spotted a perfect vee-shaped skein of wild geese heading toward some southward rendezvous.

I loved the sense of history and continuity the river bestowed on me, its breadth and depth, the persuasion of familiarity I now felt. The mountains I glimpsed in the distance fascinated me. The charts of the river illustrated contours along the water's edge, and the lines narrowed excitingly at Jones

*Homeward bound down the Hudson.*

Point where I rounded the bend past Dunderberg Mountain, then Anthony's Nose and the sheer tree-covered slopes of Storm King Mountain looming dramatically above the river.

The Palisades were etched in short lines on the chart, and these scenic, perpendicular cliffs came as a pleasant surprise, chiseled by nature and almost destroyed by man. They were dramatic in any light but most effective at dawn or sunset when they reflected warm hues from their smooth, flushed faces.

The Catskills and Helderberg Mountains loomed to the west, and we plunged into the divide of the Hudson Highlands, but I was also within the Appalachians, an exciting notion. I knew they ranged for 1500 miles from the province of Quebec to northern Alabama. Hikers tramped the Appalachian Trail for weeks of energetic trekking, but I was happy to view them from the cockpit of little *Dart*.

From the sheltered waterways, I admired the Green Mountains of Vermont, the Adirondacks of New York State, and the Laurentians of Quebec. I followed mountains wherever *Dart* took me. Sometimes, they were just a distant glimpse, mounded, misty, and mysterious. For many weeks they were invisible, but I knew they were there, just over the horizon, tucked into the vault of my mind.

A physical landscape map of my route through the waterways was a revelation. It depicted the Appalachians ridged and crumpled like the backbone of a long-dead stegosaurus, born of tectonic collision and world-shattering geological upheavals.

The peaks bordering the Hudson River estuary were shown in glorious Technicolor, from the deep blue of the winding river to pallid greens on the plains to lush auburn on the steep mountaintops—the higher the peak, the more intense the scarlet.

How narrow the river seemed on the chart, winding its way across the eroded plains, following the path of the ice age glacier that ground its way south in prehistory. The original steep peaks formed by the collision between the North American and African continents a billion years ago were eroded and smoothed, leaving only the enduring summits identified on maps and charts. My depth sounder painted a vision of underwater hills and valleys in the Hudson River, as it flickered from five feet to over 200 feet and back.

The tide influenced me constantly, either riding it or stemming it. It gave me a lift from five to eight knots or slowed me from five to two knots, an invisible force that I was unaware of until I glanced at the GPS that, via satellite, told me my speed over the ground.

If the engine stopped, the tide would have carried me onwards—or backwards—for a while anyway. When the tide turned again, I'd be carried in reverse. They say that if you just sat tight in the tide and allowed yourself to be carried back and forth, it would take 127 days to make the voyage down-river from Albany to New York.

I felt at home at the tiller, steering *Dart* quietly and competently, not nervous, no longer anxious at the thought of docking or locking. I now knew I could place *Dart* where I wanted her, and I enjoyed the feeling of mastery. Her familiar, cream colored decks formed a frame for the molten, silver surge of venerable river before me.

*Dart*'s pert nose in the air and rounded shoulders had eased their way through calms, waves, and storms. The only shelter I needed was the canvas bimini above, with my companion Tucker asleep below decks or perched on the bow, her little brown ears lifting to the breeze like tiny origami sails. Together we had ploughed a furrow through lakes and locks, canals and rivers in two summers of leisurely exploration. We visited small towns, vast cities, isolated villages, and unique communities. I learned about *Dart,* and I learned about myself.

I discovered that when an unexpected challenge arose, I was far too busy dealing with the circumstances to be afraid. I had to cope with the engine, the tiller, and the steering, and it was too late to be scared once it was over. I originally doubted my ability to manage *Dart* within a lock, and now I had hundreds of locks satisfyingly behind me. I had successfully negotiated many miles of waterway, marinas, docks, bridges, lakes, rivers, canals, thunderstorms, heat waves, rain showers, and fogs. I had lost my way, and found it again on occasion, but mostly followed a true and accurate course.

The bluffs of the gaunt, gleaming Palisades stood to attention with respect as I made my final pass. It was strange to recall that these two summer-long voyages were intended to challenge me mentally, physically, and psychologically. That's what I told myself before I set off. Now I had to read the log of past months to remind myself how scared I was at times. The night before setting off alone on the first day of my second year, I wrote, "I've just read through the cruising guide and scared myself silly at what lies ahead."

I did that? I truly don't remember, perhaps because I faced all the fears and concerns, the apprehension and qualms, and dealt with them. I just plowed on through them and emerged on the other side, stronger, braver, and ultimately proficient in survival skills. I eventually enjoyed the solitary experiences and blushed to recall the frantic calls for help and company in the early days. I just needed to conquer the trepidation and was proud now to have done so.

Tucker was curled up, napping contentedly beside me in the cockpit as I stood at the tiller and steered *Dart* under Tappan Zee Bridge, past Yonkers, heading for the George Washington Bridge.

The tide was flowing with us down the Hudson, the engine murmuring cheerfully, and the bow wave burbling.

A silvery beam of sunlight burst through the clouds, illuminating the statuesque Manhattan skyline, and through the mist, not far ahead, Liberty raised high her shining torch.

# About the Author

A war baby born in Liverpool, England, the author has childhood memories of bombers droning overhead, searchlights, and air-raid shelters. Moving to Bermuda to live with relatives, she says, was akin to flying "over the rainbow."

She is now a Bermuda citizen and writes about boating for local publications.

She and her husband George ran a glass-bottom boat in Bermuda for many years while raising three children. Now divorced, the amicable couple possess their own sailboats and may be found working or sailing on one or the other.

Gillian wrote her book, she says, to encourage others, especially mature women, to embark on a venture "before it's too late."

"Sailing around the world is not necessary," she advises. "There are plenty of adventures to be found closer to home."

# Far Horizons Media Company

## Nautical Book Imprints

Nautical Publishing Company - Bristol Fashion Publishing Company
Wescott Cove Publishing Company

### Nautical Books

Boaters' Book of Nautical Terms
Skipper's Handbook
Practical Seamanship
Captain Jack's Complete Navigation
Captain Jack's Basic Navigation
Captain Jack's Celestial Navigation
Fiberglass Boat Survey
Buying A Great Boat
Designing Power & Sail
Building A Fiberglass Boat
Boat Repair Made Easy – Haul Out
Boat Repair Made Easy – Engines
Boat Repair Made Easy – Finishes
Boat Repair Made Easy – Systems
Electronics Aboard
Ship's Log Book
Electric Propulsion for Boats
Cruising South: What to Expect Along the ICW
Lights & Legends
Simple Boat Projects

Boater's Checklist
Beach Cruising & Coastal Camping
Florida Through The Islands
Complete Guide to Diesel Marine Engines
Complete Guide to Outboard Engines
Complete Guide to Gasoline Marine Engines
Trouble Shooting Gasoline Marine Engines
Marine Weather Forecasting
Basic Boat Maintenance
Outfitting & Organizing Your Boat
Irma Quarterdeck Reports
Four Across the Atlantic
Going About!
The Last Schoonerman
White Squall: The Last Voyage of Albatross
Five Against The Sea
First Time Around
Circumnavigation, Vols. 1 & 2
Inside American Paradise
VHF Marine Radio Handbook

## Motorcycle Book Imprint

Motorcycle Publishing Company

### Motorcycle Books

Back in the Saddle Again
Upper Mississippi Valley by Motorcycle
Enjoy the Ride - A Fitness Guide for Motorcyclists

For a complete listing of all our titles, go to
www.FarHorizonsMedia.com

Far Horizons Media Company is a Division of NetPV, Inc.
P. O. Box 560989, Rockledge, FL 32956 - www.NetPV.com